Closer to God

THRIVING AFTER PAIN
AND PLATEAUS

THRIVING AFTER PAIN
AND PLATEAUS

JIM KAMINSKI

Niche Pressworks
Indianapolis, IN

For permission to reprint portions of this content or bulk purchases, contact jim@newcovenantlife.com

Published by Niche Pressworks; NichePressworks.com
Indianapolis, IN

ISBN
Hardcover: 978-1-962956-86-4
Paperback: 978-1-962956-87-1
eBook: 978-1-962956-88-8

Library of Congress Cataloging-in-Publication Data on File at lccn.loc.gov

The views expressed herein are solely those of the author and do not necessarily reflect the views of the publisher.

Author: *"Lord, I know I'm not good at marketing. Would you help me to get people to read my book?"*

Lord: *"I've been working to get people to read My book for a long time."*

Table of Contents

CHAPTER 1

You Can Move Forward Even When Faith Hurts

Journeying from Disappointment to Fulfillment

"The doctor says I have cancer."

My wife called me unexpectedly that day weeping. I was shocked and angry that the doctor had given her this dreadful diagnosis without me at her side. She had seen him for a biopsy the week before, and then suddenly he called her into his office to give her the lab results. I would later learn that a fourteen-month nightmare had begun.

My wife had noticed multiple breast lumps over the previous few years, but they all had just gone away. She decided to have the doctor look at one to stop fighting all the fear in her mind. Her mammogram that fall had shown no problems, so within five months, something had changed terribly.

We were both in our early fifties, had enjoyed thirty-one years of a very happy marriage and seven years of pastoring a church, and had raised five beautiful children. We enjoyed them immensely and did all the soccer and basketball practices each year. I was sure this disease was not God's will for us. My mother-in-law had often commented, "You two are the most compatible couple I've ever seen." I didn't want our love story to end.

The oncologist sadly advised my wife, "You have an 11 percent chance of beating this and a 22 percent chance if we try various chemotherapy and steroid treatments." I remember waking up in the morning and, for thirty seconds, feeling refreshed and ready for a new day. Then the painful reality would slap me in the face, and I would groan and sigh deeply. Every day I felt the weight of this burden choking the life out of my precious wife and me as well.

We did all the things pastors had taught us over thirty-five years. We wrote out pages of Bible promises and read them out loud. We made confessions that she was healed. We called prayer lines. It seemed we would take one step forward when she would feel better, and then she went two steps back.

Doctors gave her steroids after the disease spread to her spine. Those shots affected her mind, and physically, she felt hot. One day she bolted out of the patio door and crawled on bare hands and knees to fall into the pool to cool off. I brought her back inside and tended to her bleeding hands and knees. Then I went sobbing to the hardware store to get alarms that screamed when anyone opened an exterior door. Was this the way life was supposed to go for pastors who served God the best they knew? Have you ever prayed for something with all your heart, only to feel that God was silent?

At one point my wife said, "I want to go to the side that has the bigger party." I knew what that

Was this the way life was supposed to go for pastors who served God the best they knew?

meant. How could the family and I compete with a heavenly welcome? We posted a picture of all our grandchildren next to her bed in a desperate attempt to feed her desire to stay here.

Her parents paid for naturopathic cocktails to help fight the awful disease. During one of these treatments, her vitals dropped dangerously. EMTs rushed her to the hospital emergency room, where she did not recover. Our fourteen months of holding on to a slippery slope of hope were over. I was shattered in the inevitable moment when I had to reluctantly let her go. My parting words to her were, "Thank you, my Love, for thirty-two years of heaven on earth."

FACING A TEMPEST

So began the worst test of my life. My soul was in a tempest. In addition to the passing of my precious wife, my grief was amplified by other losses. I had retired from my steady twenty-seven-year career and laid down my ministry after pastoring for seven years. I no longer had my wife's significant income, and my youngest son, my last child, had just moved out to be married. Our two-story house suddenly felt extremely large, and my footsteps echoed in the emptiness. My soul felt unmoored, like a boat drifting away from shore.

My grief was profound. I was angry at God, and I told Him so in no uncertain terms. I questioned Him vehemently: "Why should I ever pray to You again when You didn't answer my most important prayer? Where were You when I needed You most? Why didn't You do what You promised?"

I let it all out, and even though I was a pastor, I remember I used a few curse words to express what I felt deeply in my soul. I waited a moment. I wasn't sure what I expected next from Him, but He did not appear to be disturbed or angry with me or even concerned with my character as a pastor. Nevertheless, I vowed, "I won't be praying to You anymore for the rest of my life."

I did not know how powerfully the moorings I had lost had anchored my peace and happiness. I told one of my kids, "I don't know what I am here for. I lost everything of value." Within thirty minutes, all five children called and reassured me, "Dad, your life matters."

The questions came rushing in: Why did this happen? Does God not answer prayers, or did I fail because I didn't have enough faith? First, I could not bring myself to think God makes mistakes, and secondly, I knew I couldn't take the hit for causing my wife's death through my lack of faith. Losing the love of my life hurt immensely. What was worse was feeling like I had lost my God too. This was a trial beyond anything I could have fathomed. The enemy wanted me to be a casualty of faith without destiny and hope, believing that God had forever forsaken me and that prayer had failed.

> *Losing the love of my life hurt immensely. What was worse was feeling like I had lost my God too.*

KEEPING THE FAITH

Fast forward five years, and I found myself living closer to God, having daily joy, and praying ten times as much as I had before this experience. How did that happen? Why did my spiritual life not crash and burn as others did? One couple I know ended up divided over a type 1 diabetes diagnosis. The husband became bitter and left God, but the wife clung to Him. I talked with a man who told me he had lost his thirty-year-old son to drug addiction. He and his wife nearly lost their faith over it, but they came out stronger than before. What makes the difference? Here's what I discovered through that season.

God wants you, dear reader, to continue to grow through problems. Christ spoke promises to sustain you through pain and plateaus and to bring you into a better place and a vibrant daily walk with Him. Jesus said in Matthew 7 that storms and winds come against all houses — our lives — and the ones that endure are those who keep His sayings. We shall see that it's not big exploits, but many small actions that are needed to produce a strong life. The following chapters are a guide to grow closer to God, to be healed, and to move forward in purpose and destiny.

DISCOVERING WHAT IS HINDERING YOU

What is hindering your increase in God is *not* a mystery. Jesus told us where to look for the causes of failure. In the parable of the sower (Mark 4:13-20), He gives us a simple explanation why some people are fruitful and some are not.

What is hindering your increase in God is not a mystery.

Jesus used the stony ground to represent mishandled trials and persecutions that often cause people to fall away. If you feel like God abandoned you in your time of deepest need — a big loss in finances, disease, ruined relationships, church hurts, broken promises, shattered dreams, or death of a loved one, like me — don't lose heart. Together, we will discover the path of return to God.

But first we must deal with the sneaky weeds that choke life out of a plant that is otherwise designed for fruitfulness. See if you can find yourself in these signs that point to a plateaued or stalled Christian life or unhealed wounds.

Signs of a plateaued life

- Does your Christian life feel like the *Groundhog Day* movie where it's a series of the same day?
- Do you feel frustrated and unfulfilled because your religious activity does not satisfy your soul? You go to more services, more Bible studies, and more seminars, but somehow, you're not any closer to God than you were ten years ago.
- Do you find yourself saying, "There has to be more to God than this. Why am I still sighing and crying? Why wasn't my new church better?" Are you wondering, "What am I missing?"
- Do you consider what other spiritually mature Christians have that you don't? Are you asking, "What do I need to know or do to grow closer to God?"
- Has it been a while since you received a new understanding of Jesus Christ?

If you answered yes to any of these questions, perhaps you are stalled. But take heart, it's possible to move forward and grow closer to God. You will need to believe and embrace fully the following three truths.

1. *God wants you to grow in Christ more than you want it.*

My story tells how God taught me this truth. If you think God might not want something for you, you won't believe He will do it. One day I was pleading with God to make me holy. "Please make me Christlike! You know I want it! Please do it as I am seriously hungry for You." I sensed His rebuke: "You are acting like you want this more than I do." I knew instantly that I was blaming Him for my failures. I was also pridefully thinking that I had a greater desire for God than He did for me! My faith grew when I humbled myself to trust His desire above mine. "He leads me in the paths of righteousness for His name's sake" (Psalm 23:3).

2. The normal Christian experience is to be changed from one degree of glory to another, by the power of the Holy Spirit.

The Apostle Paul describes us this way: "But we all, with unveiled face, beholding as in a mirror the glory of the Lord, are being transformed into the same image from glory to glory, just as by the Spirit of the Lord" (2 Corinthians 3:18). God is faithful to do this in us as we look at Him. Plateauing is not normal; it indicates a problem.

3. To grow as a Christian, you must be intentional.

In his book The 15 Invaluable Laws of Growth[1], John Maxwell asserts that we hold a big misconception that personal growth is automatic. We think that since our bodies naturally grew from conception to adulthood, our personal Christian growth will be the same. But the truth is that we must be intentional to grow. If a child does not walk after one year or talk after two, we know something might be amiss, and we take action. We must admit that something needs to change if we are not growing closer to God. Then we must take steps to adjust our lives. Your pastor does not have the time and resources to cause all the flock to grow, but the Holy Spirit does, and that is why Jesus sent Him.

THE GOOD NEWS

God has provision in the New Covenant to bring you from frustration to a faithful, confident, and unshakeable supernatural life in the center of Christ. This book is designed to help you with that. First, we must uncover what is hindering your spiritual growth, and then we will talk about the change from "how-to" to "who-to." From there, we will learn how to hear God's voice and talk with Him every day.

This is your time to move forward! Your Savior wants it! Others may have made friends with the status quo, but you can't. You're the only one who can be the hero in your story. Even if you are on a plateau in life, you must not stop pursuing more life in Jesus. Dear one, the best thing about the pain you are feeling is finding Jesus as your answer! He meant it more deeply than we know when He said that He is our way, our truth, and our life (John 14:6).

Satan is the father of lies, and they are his best evil weapon. In the next chapter, I have picked out some of the most insidious and harmful lies for us to recognize and conquer.

"But I have prayed for you, that your faith should not fail;
and when you have returned to Me, strengthen your brethren."

— Jesus, in Luke 22:32

Section One

WHAT HAPPENED?

CHAPTER 2

Lies Get You Stuck, but Truth Sets You Free

Unlearning Lies That Hurt You More Than You Know

When I was eleven years old, my mother died after a long bout with breast cancer. I had nine siblings, and ten children losing their mother is quite a tragedy, but only the priest wept and wailed at the funeral. Oddly, no one in my family seemed to grieve. No one talked about it or asked questions. I remember looking at my brothers and sisters and thinking, "I'm going to be okay," but I really wasn't.

What I didn't realize was that I was trying to fill an emptiness after losing my mother. Going to church to pray every day helped me to connect with something bigger. When I look back on it now, I see that God was reaching out to me to connect with *someone* bigger — to bring me closer to Himself.

In the two years after my mother died, I attended Catholic Mass every day at 6:45 a.m. as a sixth and seventh grader. I treasured those quiet moments in the cavernous church where I talked to God and asked Him if He wanted me to become a priest. No rain, sleet, snow, cold, or heat caused me to miss this meeting with God. Only a few pious elderly women were there on those holy mornings.

I wanted to be like the priest because he was close to God. He celebrated the Mass and even held the communion host of His Presence in his hands. I remember asking God to show me if I should be a priest by making a spot on the wall move before my very eyes. It never happened! After eighth grade, I met with the seminary representative to discuss entering in the fall to begin the path to priesthood. I decided, however, to wait until after high school since I figured by then I would know if I would become interested in girls. (I knew priests could not be married.)

In my sophomore year of high school, a cute girl let me know through the grapevine that she wanted to go to the dance with me. I was terrified since I knew I couldn't dance, but I asked her, and she enchanted me with her intelligent conversation. After a movie date the next week, I walked her to her front door and said a nervous "thank you." Then, as I was about to make my escape, she said, "Well, if you aren't going to, then I will." She kissed me, and you could say it was the kiss that killed the priest(hood). I instantly knew I wasn't going to be a priest! Sadly, I also believed the lie that I could no longer be one of God's special people who were close to Him. This story illustrates the #1 lie discussed later in this chapter.

PLATEAU-MAKERS

Obvious attacks like big losses and problems with our health or income are dangerous, but probably worse are the subtle lies that seek to keep us away from God. These are often delivered to us in a religious message, ritual, or activity. I call them plateau-makers. When you are plateauing, you lose a live connection with God. There is no heart-to-heart, and you just go through the motions. You aren't saying no to God, but there is a vital disconnect. It's not an out-and-out rebellion, but a lot of doubts and fears come in. Then you encounter a challenge and begin to think, "I don't know Him like I thought I did."

I'm here to identify these plateau-makers as roaches crawling in the dark night of our minds to consume our spiritual food. I want to shine the light on them, so they flee or get stomped to death.

THE FREEDOM TEST

I created a graph of my spiritual life to illustrate the effect of lies and truth on our growth. As an enlightening exercise, I suggest you take time now to write a timeline of your Christian experience. Show plateau times, big trials, and times of good growth. Note what churches, persons, books, and trials are associated with your graph movement.

When you look at my graph, you can see that canceling religious lies produced the biggest increase in my life with God. The truths that canceled these lies brought me freedom and became the framework for this book. Major lies are listed in this chapter, and others will become evident in subsequent chapters.

Canceling religious lies produced the biggest increase in my life with God.

Jim's Christian Life Graph

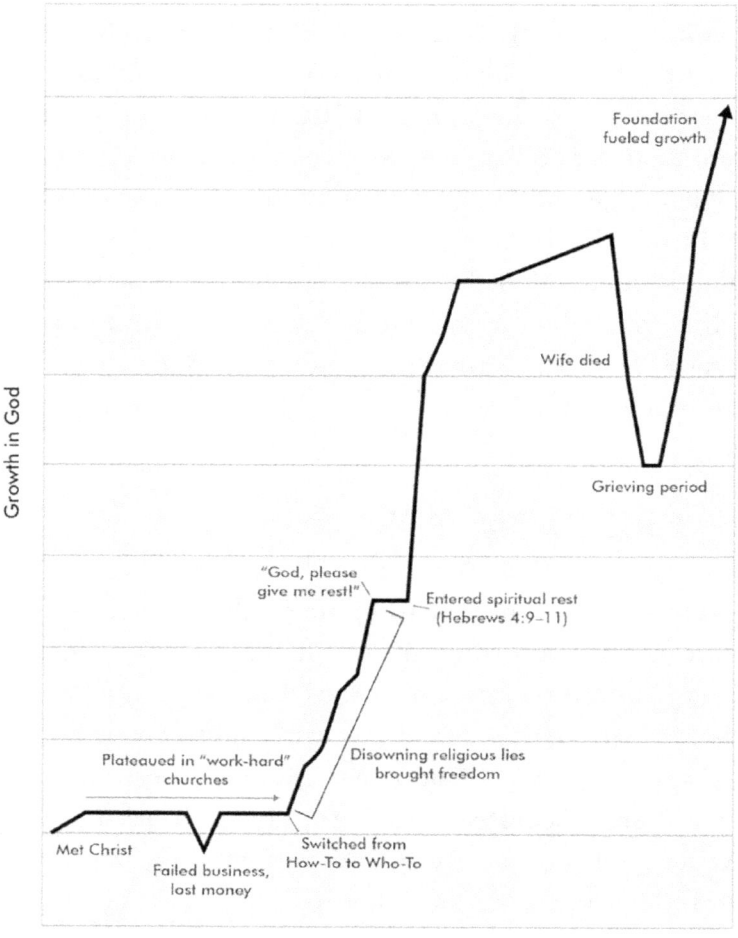

Growth in God

Foundation fueled growth

Wife died

Grieving period

"God, please give me rest!"

Entered spiritual rest (Hebrews 4:9–11)

Plateaued in "work-hard" churches

Disowning religious lies brought freedom

Met Christ

Failed business, lost money

Switched from How-To to Who-To

Years

Some lies are overt, while others are subtle. Lies have one goal — to keep us from experiencing freedom in God. This "freedom litmus test" is a major key that God uses to train us to recognize lies. In John 8:32 Jesus said, "And you shall know the truth, and the truth shall make you free." We don't have to remain stuck in a lie; Jesus told us to abide in His Word and experience freedom.

Here's the advice I wish someone had given me earlier in my Christian life: it's important to be ready to *unlearn*. We have thoughts about religion and God's Word from tradition or education, and some of these are our greatest hindrances to spiritual growth. Even though Christian ministers and culture mean well, I must tell you, we have all likely swallowed some untruths about God and His goodness. Let's unlearn the lies, embrace truth, and grow.

Lie #1: Only special Christians can be really close to God.

Truth: God wants intimacy more than you do.

"God doesn't want me to bother Him with this."

"I wonder what it's like for Sister Spiritual when she prays. Does she feel God all the time?"

"I bet Pastor hears from God every day."

Many Christians act like God is distant, even if they wouldn't necessarily say this aloud. We think He's far away and hard to talk to or hear from. He expects us to muddle along and do our best, and somehow it might be enough. Some of us have been subtly trained to believe that it's difficult to get close to God, and thus, only a few very special people get to be close to Him. Brother Been-There at church advised us that growing close to Christ is rare.

Sometimes we act like the Holy Spirit holds a lottery, and some Christians win, and some don't. We look at the Christian minister and think, "Wow, the minister won the Christian lottery, and he gets to be close to God and to know how to pray and to hear from God. But my lottery ticket didn't win. God just left me on the sidelines as a spectator." This is not true, my friend. God wants us close to Him, and we can have as much of Him as we want. Say instead, "I won the Christian lottery. I got the biggest, highest prize — God's own Son Jesus Christ!" Remember the following promise: "Draw near to God and He will draw near to you" (James 4:8).

God is the one who wants to have a close, intimate relationship with us, and He wants it even more than we do! He made a way to adopt us as His children and for Him to be our Daddy (*Abba* in Hebrew). Galatians 4:6 says, "And because you are sons, God has sent forth the Spirit of His Son into your hearts, crying out, 'Abba, Father!'" Scripture also tells us, "Jesus answered and said to him, 'If anyone loves Me, he will keep My word; and My Father will love him, and We will come to him and make Our home with him'" (John 14:23). Jesus reiterated this in John 17:26, saying, "And I have declared to them Your name, and will declare it, that the love with which You loved Me may be in them, and I in them." God makes His home in us; you can't get any closer than that!

Matthew 1:23 quotes Isaiah 7:14: "Behold, the virgin shall be with child, and bear a Son, and they shall call His name Immanuel," which translates to "God with us." That doesn't mean God is somewhere on the earth, floating around somewhere in your neighborhood. It means He is in you. Jesus assured His disciples that we would be in Him, and He would be in us. "At that day you will know that I am in My Father, and you in Me, and I in you" (John 14:20). That day has come because Jesus finished His mission, left the earth, and sent His Spirit to us just like He said He would.

I did not know when I was a young man contemplating the priesthood that I was already eligible to be as close to God as possible — I just needed to enter a relationship with God through Jesus. Let's demolish the lie that there are "special" Christians who have a different level of relationship with God. We are all God's children, and He gives of Himself freely to every one of us.

Here's a prayer to use to kill this plateau-maker: "Father, forgive me for believing that You show favoritism. I reject that evil thought, and I rejoice in Your desire and power that are active to draw me close. Thank You."

Lie #2: The minister's work is holy; yours is worldly.

Truth: Your whole life is holy.

It wasn't until my freshman year of college that I finally met Jesus. Instantly, I knew why I had been born — to live for God. I became immersed in reading the Bible every day and went to every Christian meeting I could. But my plateau was coming. I had swallowed another plateau-maker somewhere along the way. It was this: "Only pastors and people on the stage can do the sacred work. Everything I do is mundane. I paint, teach children, do carpentry, or program computers. I don't qualify to be a minister because all my work is secular and not good enough." This one lie has persisted for years, even centuries, in the church. So sad!

What is holy work?

One morning I was leaving to do my errands for the day. My neighbor called me over and asked if I could help him put on a spare tire. Being newly immigrated from Africa, he knew nothing about the process, so I helped him on his way. As he neared the tire shop, his spare blew out. They quoted him $170 to replace it. I told him not to do it, and I found one for $50 at a junkyard. He told me that I just helped Jesus put on a spare tire, and I helped Him save $120 that day! He explained by quoting

Matthew 25:40: "And the King will answer and say to them, 'Assuredly, I say to you, inasmuch as you did it to one of the least of these My brethren, you did it to Me.'"

Yes, we must have dedicated prayer and fellowship time with God, but God sees our whole life in Him. Our caring for others and our daily work are also time with God.

How does the Bible say to look at your work? Colossians 3:23–24 is clear: "And whatever you do, do it heartily, as to the Lord and not to men, knowing that from the Lord you will receive the reward of the inheritance; for you serve the Lord Christ." Whatever you do, wherever you work or serve, you do it for Him. Everything you do is sacred to God. The job that allows you to give is part of your holy life. Peter wrote in his first epistle that you are "a holy priesthood" (1 Peter 2:5). Notice he didn't say you do the work of priests, but instead that you *are* priests. Your whole life is set apart to God to know Him, to love Him, and — out of that love — to serve Him.

I heard a prayer from a good pastor who loves people, loves God, and wants everybody to grow. But the prayer went like this: "God, I'm thankful we can spend a moment in Your presence when we're here in Your house." This kind of prayer implies that God is not present in me when I am outside the church building.

Though we love it when God's people assemble publicly, and God is a very special presence there, we would do well to remember that we are always God's house. The Bible says your body is the temple of God in 1 Corinthians 6:19: "Or do you not know that your body is the temple of the Holy Spirit who is in you, whom you have from God, and you are not your own?" You're always in God's house, because you *are* His house. In fact, the Greek word for temple in this verse is *naos*, and it is the one used for the Holy of Holies in the Jewish temple — the part of the temple where God's presence was and where no one could go except one priest once a year under special circumstances. You are this dwelling place of God now. Remember: the veil in the temple was torn in two from top to bottom when Jesus died. He opened the way for God's sacred presence to be in His children.

If you see that you have believed the lie that your activities are not as spiritual or important as others' activities, act now. Stomp on this belief by saying out loud, "I am *not* believing that lie anymore, and I am stating that every endeavor of mine serves God's kingdom and is for Him!"

Lie #3: Life is too busy, and there never seems to be enough time to be with God.

Truth: You have as much time as anyone and everyone else.

In Mark 4:19, Jesus said, "and the cares of this world, the deceitfulness of riches, and the desires for other things entering in choke the word and it becomes unfruitful." Did He at all want this to be your life? No. He was pointing out the possibility that the good news of this Christian life could be starved out if your attention was on other things.

The story of the wedding feast invitation in Luke 14, told by Jesus a long time ago, notes the outcome of being too busy for God:

> Now when one of those who sat at the table with Him heard these things, he said to Him, "Blessed is he who shall eat bread in the kingdom of God!" Then He said to him, "A certain man gave a great supper and invited many, and sent his servant at supper time to say to those who were invited, 'Come, for all things are now ready.' But they all with one accord began to make excuses. The first said to him, 'I have bought a piece of ground, and

I must go and see it. I ask you to have me excused.' And another said, 'I have bought five yoke of oxen, and I am going to test them. I ask you to have me excused'. Still another said, 'I have married a wife, and therefore I cannot come.' So that servant came and reported these things to his master. Then the master of the house, being angry, said to his servant, 'Go out quickly into the streets and lanes of the city, and bring in here the poor and the maimed and the lame and the blind.' And the servant said, 'Master, it is done as you commanded, and still there is room.' Then the master said to the servant, 'Go out into the highways and hedges, and compel them to come in, that my house may be filled. For I say to you that none of those men who were invited shall taste my supper.'" (Luke 14:15–24)

Notice all three men rejected God's invitation to dine with His Son based on a busyness excuse. This ought to concern us. The cares of this life took priority over the Master. Look at His response. He was angry, and He said none of those busy ones would taste His supper! It matters to Him personally how you spend your time, and it matters for you. You don't lose precious time when you spend it with God; instead, you gain much.

Another aspect of this story to encourage you is that Jesus says you can still get into the wedding feast even if you are broken. You may be lacking in resources (poor), wholeness (maimed), ability (lame), or vision (blind), but God's message is still for you. His invitation carries

> *Notice all three men rejected God's invitation to dine with His Son based on a busyness excuse.*

authority to get you all the way into the wedding feast of eternal life. Now you can say, "Yes, Lord, I accept Your invitation to be with You at Your wedding feast, in Your house, in Your kingdom."

If you believe you are too busy to spend time with God, you will continue to live on the plateau and go nowhere. If you believe God is desirable, if He is a high priority, then you will keep company with Him. You're not too busy for what you *want* to do — you allocate time for those things. You could try telling your spouse you are too busy to spend time with them. How would that go? Doesn't God feel the same? Make a radical change to escape the busyness excuse by repeating this honest prayer: "God, I have not prioritized You today or even this week. I now choose to reset my priorities and give You the attention You deserve."

Lie #4: You will always be a sinner; your heart is wicked.

Truth: Christ came to free us from sin by giving us a new heart.

Imagine being in a Saturday evening meeting listening to the Apostle Paul. He would greet his audience, "Good evening, saints!" Then he would follow with:

> I thank my God always concerning you for the grace of God which was given to you by Christ Jesus...so that you come short in no gift, eagerly waiting for the revelation of our Lord Jesus Christ, who will also confirm you to the end, that you may be blameless in the day of our Lord Jesus Christ. God is faithful, by whom you were called into the fellowship of His Son, Jesus Christ our Lord. (1 Corinthians 1:4-9)

His words of assurance, God's promise to keep you blameless, and God's faithfulness to you would roll around in your mind all night. Then on Sunday morning, you might go to a Christian church and hear the preacher say, "We're all just sinners, and we always will be." What?! Was Paul mistaken when he called the Corinthians, Colossians, and Ephesians "saints," or when he said Christ would confirm us blameless in the day of the Lord? You would find yourself forced to agree either with Paul or with the preacher.

The problem with believing you are a sinner by nature, even as a Christian, is that it convinces you that you will naturally sin all the time because of forces beyond your control — that God has made no provision to overcome sin. This is a heart-breaking prospect for anyone who loves Jesus. May you not at least hope that you can grow closer to God in joyful obedience? Did He really make you a new creation? It is not in God's heart to cleanse you from your sins and then tell you you're still a sinner and must keep sinning.

A Christian's heart is not desperately wicked.

Many modern preachers refer to Jeremiah 17:9 for the idea that we are sinners because our hearts are wicked. The verse says, "The heart is deceitful above all things, and desperately wicked; Who can know it?" The problem with this is that it is a misapplication. This was spoken to the rebellious kingdom of Judah. And how rebellious were they? So bad that God told Jeremiah three times not to pray for these people (Jeremiah 7:16, 11:14, 14:11)! "Then the LORD said to me, 'Even if Moses and Samuel stood before Me, My mind would not be favorable toward this people'" (Jeremiah 15:1). This is the context in which he wrote that their heart was deceitful above all things and wicked. This was not intended for Christians today who are under the New

Covenant made by Jesus. There is no place in the New Testament where God told us to quit praying for ourselves or for others.

Read God's New Covenant promise: "I will give you a new heart and put a new spirit within you; I will take the heart of stone out of your flesh and give you a heart of flesh. I will put My Spirit within you and cause you to walk in My statutes, and you will keep My judgments and do them" (Ezekiel 36:26–27). Read more about your new heart under the New Covenant in chapter 8.

Jesus purposely identified His death as bringing in the New Covenant: "Likewise He also took the cup after supper, saying, 'This cup is the new covenant in My blood, which is shed for you'" (Luke 22:20). God made it clear He will give you a new heart. That is what you have as a believer. This transformation happens in the New Covenant. "Therefore, if anyone is in Christ, he is a new creation; old things have passed away; behold, all things have become new" (2 Corinthians 5:17).

I'm sorry that you were probably told the lie that your heart is wicked and deceitful. Now is the time to sever that lie by praying: "Father, I reject the lie that my heart is wicked. I thank You for putting a new, good heart in me according to Your promise. Help me to more fully understand that Jesus brought me into the New Covenant."

Lie #5: Lukewarm Christianity is okay because we're safe from hell.

Truth: A Christian constantly grows to be more Christlike.

Have you heard the following sentiments or even held them yourself?

"As long as I know my sins are forgiven and know I'm going to heaven, then I'm probably alright."

"I think I'm safe enough from hell because God can't expect too much of imperfect humans."

I highly recommend the book *The Sacred Romance*, wherein authors John Eldredge and Brent Curtis claim that we have settled for a "less-wild lover" than our hearts cry out for.[2] If each of us really listened to our soul, we would know with certainty that, yes, we want more than "safe."

A common practice among God's children is to compare ourselves with each other. We look at the Christians who have attended church for ten, twenty, or thirty years, and our spiritual level is as good as theirs. However, Brother Been-There and Sister Status-Quo may have settled for

> *If each of us really listened to our soul, we would know with certainty that, yes, we want more than "safe."*

a routine Christian life, and they are not our finest role models. Hopefully you can't settle for being a humdrum Christian. That's why you're reading this book.

Dear ones, comparing ourselves with others in church will keep us on the plateau. Our aim is to be like Jesus. How close are you to being like Jesus? In Romans 8:29, this great truth is presented: we are "predestined to be conformed to the image of His Son, that He might be the firstborn among many brethren." Our comparison is to what Jesus acted like, thought like, and spoke like. Paul said, "Imitate me, just as I also imitate Christ" (1 Corinthians 11:1). The calling is the same for us. In Luke 6:40, Jesus Himself said the "disciple is not above his teacher, but everyone who is perfectly trained will be like his teacher."

One book spurred me to accept this calling, and I highly recommend it. *Like Christ* by Andrew Murray[3] includes thirty-one chapters on how God expects us to be like Christ. This book birthed something in me. I was surprised at the many ways in which God tells us we are made to be like Christ. I came to the place where I surrendered and said, "God, I must be like Christ. I don't have the power to do it. I know that You do. No offense, Lord, I love Your people, but I can't be like 95 percent of them. They're not close enough to You. I am ready to go anywhere, read anything, follow anyone that can change me. I must be conformed to the image of Your Son Jesus." His reply was essentially, "I will do it in you since you asked, but you will take some time!"

It is very possible we have heard (and believed) fellow Christians who have told us that status quo Christian living should be expected. Brother Been-There and Sister Seen-It-All say it's all okay, we don't get too excited. Our Christian life is all covered by some kind of grace that makes it okay that we are not changing too much. Contrary to this, Jesus said in John 15:2 and 8, "Every branch in Me that does not bear fruit He takes away... By this My Father is glorified, that you bear much fruit." Why would we want to allow any part of our life to stagnate and be barren? Jesus expects us to let Him be our vine, our life-source and example, so that we look more and more like Him.

The normal Christian experience is to be changed from good to better, glory to glory, not from glory to plateau to fruit-lessness. 2 Corinthians 3:7–9 says:

> But if the ministry of death, written and engraved on stones, was glorious, so that the children of Israel could not look steadily at the face of Moses because of the glory of his countenance, which glory was passing away, how will the ministry of the Spirit not be more glorious? For if the ministry of condemnation had glory, the ministry of righteousness exceeds much more in glory.

The Holy Spirit lives in us to work (minister) glory in us. Think of it! Glory reflects God's substance and worth, and that is what the Holy Spirit works in us. Jesus gifted us His Spirit to be our teacher, encourager, coach, and power to change.

It bears repeating that the normal Christian life is to be progressing from one degree of glory to another. You have one degree of shining out Christ's life in your life, and then you grow to another degree of Christlikeness. That's the normal life — anything else is abnormal. If your children aren't growing, you get concerned. If your son is two years old and not walking yet, you think something's wrong, and you go to the doctor. If you're not growing as Christians, it's time to admit something's wrong and take action. Pray right now: "Father, I repent for choosing to stay comfortable instead of sacrificing my comfort and becoming more like Jesus in every way. Holy Spirit, change me."

Read the encouragement from Deuteronomy 30:11. God said, "For this commandment which I command you today is not too mysterious for you, nor is it far off." This is not too hard for you. It's not too far away. It doesn't cost too much money. It's very near you — as near as the air you breathe and the sunlight that shines abundantly on you every day. You can make these changes with your Savior's effective help. You can reject the plateau-maker lies. In the next chapter, we will trade stumbling blocks for stepping stones.

"And you shall know the truth, and the truth shall make you free."

— Jesus, in John 8:32

CHAPTER 3

Trials Are Like a Lost Ax Head

Recovering Your Cutting Edge

In explaining the parable of the sower and the seed, Jesus revealed why some people lose their way. "These likewise are the ones sown on stony ground who, when they hear the word, immediately receive it with gladness; and they have no root in themselves, and so endure only for a time. Afterward, when tribulation or persecution arises for the word's sake, immediately they stumble" (Mark 4:16–17). The following story shows the steps to reopen the door to your closer walk with God after a trial.

YOUR CUTTING EDGE: A STORY OF RECOVERY

In 2 Kings 6:1–7, the prophet Elisha helps a man find his ax head:

And the sons of the prophets said to Elisha, "See now, the place where we dwell with you is too small for us. Please, let us go to the Jordan, and let every man take a beam from there, and let us make there a place where we may dwell." So he answered, "Go." Then one said, "Please consent to go with your servants." And he answered, "I will go." So he went with them. And when they came to the Jordan, they cut down trees. But as one was cutting down a tree, the iron ax head fell into the water; and he cried out and said, "Alas, master! For it was borrowed!" So the man of God said, "Where did it fall?" And he showed him the place. So he cut off a stick, and threw it in there; and he made the iron float. Therefore he said, "Pick it up for yourself." So he reached out his hand and took it.

First, the man had lost his ax head, which symbolizes the power to act productively in life. Your ax head symbolizes your cutting edge — your ability to make a difference, to do some work, and to move things.

Then the prophet said, "Where did it fall?" Our first step is to go back and remember where we lost some of our zeal for God or our trust in God. Look for the place where your ax head was lost, and He will show you where it happened. He will be with you as you revisit your painful place of loss.

Next, the prophet commanded, "Pick it up." Your trial did not cause you to lose your cutting edge permanently — it's not really lost forever. "For the gifts and the calling of God are irrevocable" (Romans 11:29). God will float it back up for you to see, just like He caused the ax head to float so the man could reach out and take it. It's waiting for you. You must make the move to reach out and take it back.

In this chapter, we're going to look at past trials and choose to see them as God sees them. We will be able to recover our ability to function in hope and walk productively. Now is your time to identify what troubling experience caused you to stumble, see God's interpretation of it, and choose His perspective to be your own.

FAULTY RESPONSES TO TRIALS

If I had to restart my Christian journey from scratch, here's exactly what I would have wanted to know: trials come with your choice to swallow a lie or to grow in God. Jesus said, "Enter by the narrow gate; for wide is the gate and broad is the way that leads to destruction, and there are many who go in by it. Because narrow is the gate and difficult is the way which leads to life, and there are few who find it" (Matthew 7:13–14). The word *narrow* is better translated as *compressed* or *pressured* from the original Greek language. It is rendered differently in some Bible versions, but the best is *pressurized*, and that's the gate we want to enter. Thankfully, we can go back and fix situations where we took the broad road. Understand that growth comes from challenges, not easy paths.

Let's look at some big losses, such as loss of health and loss of money, that are often misinterpreted and cause a rift in our relationship with God. Notice various ways God was faithful to rearrange the meaning of losses for the people mentioned in the following stories.

Trials come with your choice to swallow a lie or to grow in God.

Loss of health

Beth (not her real name) was a tornado of activity — a pastor's wife who was busy serving and raising two children, her heart postured to serve God's people in the church along with her husband. Then came the day she experienced a rollover car accident on the interstate and sustained severe whiplash that changed life as she knew it.

With two children at home, she was unable to care for them and found herself needing time away from them to recover and heal. At church she had to sit in the back with her big neck brace, and she required an escort in and out. She was unable to return to her pastoral duties for a long time. Ironically, right before the rollover she had listened to a message entitled "Peace in the Midst of Chaos."

Here's how Beth described that time: "I felt like a madwoman wearing the large neck brace while walking in the cul-de-sac in our neighborhood. My hair was plopped up in a messy bun, I had no makeup on, and the enemy whispered that he would end my life. He wanted to bring fear to paralyze me and render me ineffective in the kingdom. I realized I had functioned in the belief that my relationship with God was based on what I could *do* for God. Now I was hanging on by a thread and could do nothing!"

Questions exploded in Beth's mind: "Now that I am unable to function and serve as before, am I still valuable to God? Am I worth anything to Him as His child?" All she had were three passages of Scripture that she literally believed were life or death for her: Psalms 23, 27, and 91. These passages spoke life to her value as His precious child, not in what she had accomplished.

As a result of processing this trial, Beth realized her value in God was not based on her functions but in her identity in Him. First, she remembered she was still created in God's image. A car accident, her inability to serve the church, and her pause in caring for her family never changed that. While she was considering this trial, God led her to see how important her identity is to Him and to her. Beth learned that each of us must first establish our own identity as His child, which develops intimacy, and then the service we do for Him grows out of that.

Have you allowed what others think or expect of you to cause you to devalue your own identity before your Father in heaven?

Loss of money

Here is another example of a common trial. When I was in my thirties, I had a house paid for, and I borrowed money against the equity to start a business. Within two years, I lost $50,000, which was a lot of money at the time. My wife had to begin working outside the home even though we had three small children. I was hurt, and I was mad. I was told God would always take care of me. And I said, "God, I feel like you haven't taken care of me." I thought like this: my head says I can't blame God, but everything from my head down says He did fail me. My emotions would not stop screaming.

At that time, a friend of mine stepped in to help me. My wonderful friend Bernie, a man I had led to Christ, called me every day to make sure that he didn't lose his friend to this problem. God bless him. He's gone on to his reward in heaven, and I have always been thankful for what he did. I listened to my friend when he said, "God can make the sun to shine again." Over the course of some time, God *did* make the sun shine again. I recovered from that loss and did not stay angry at God. I had to humble myself, and I learned it was my own actions that led to my loss.

When an acquaintance of yours encounters a big loss, it is a serious turning point in their life. Don't underestimate the power and the importance of coming alongside them to help them through. Don't let them face it alone. If you are the one suffering, humble yourself to allow someone in to help you and offer a listening ear.

Church hurt

This story will be echoed by many Christians. Dolores (not her real name) wanted to serve in her church, but she felt rejected by leadership. She didn't have enough letters or degrees after her name, and she hadn't gone to Bible college. She kept asking to serve but was not placed. How did she react to this problem? She moved to a new church about every few years. But guess what? The same thing happened again.

Dolores would go to a church, and no one would greet her, or the pastor's wife wouldn't let her join the "in crowd." She didn't see God moving and active in churches as she expected. She began to dislike church, and her attendance fell off. She started losing her fire for God. Eventually, she almost completely gave up and plateaued in her Christian life. Dolores learned that she was blaming others for her own plateauing.

Church hurt often produces an identity crisis, and it is a time to establish your personal value to God. Ask the Holy Spirit to guide you into freedom from your hurts. Seek out a Christian counselor. After painful hurts in church, I read the Gene Edwards book *Crucified by Christians.*[4] It helped me through my own church identity crisis.

I learned to face the reality that my soul was damaged when somebody slighted me or didn't invite me or ignored me. I realized that David said in Psalm 23:3, "He restores my soul." That's when I began to practice in prayer, saying something like, "God, my friends hurt me, and my soul was damaged when I was not invited to serve. I hear that You are the one who restores souls. I'm asking You to restore my soul because it has been damaged."

He will do it. He did it for me. God wants us to grow right where we feel pressured or hurt and don't know what to do. Today's frustrating problem is the cutting edge to your growth in God right now.

Unforgiveness

Let's talk about another common source of falling away. The story of the unforgiving servant in Matthew 18:21–35 is about a servant who was forgiven about $1 million, and then he would not forgive someone else about $100. Jesus plainly said that we must forgive others if we want to be forgiven ourselves. If it's difficult to forgive, find a good book about it. Ask God to help you learn to forgive. We're going to talk in a later chapter about how to get used to talking with God about everything. You don't have to do this forgiving alone or in your own strength; ask Him for help. Talk to some others who have done it. You must deal with this issue before you can begin to grow again.

My own story about the power of forgiveness happened through a book I read that encouraged Christians to stir up the gift of God that's been given to us. There was one chapter about identifying people who had hindered your personal development. The exercise was to write down the names of all the people you could think of who had hindered your growth in God — personally, financially, or in any way. Then write a letter to one of them. So, I started to write a list. I figured I'd think of four or five people. I got twenty-six names, including my children! I was shocked. I surprised myself when I thought, "I'm not going to write to one of them; I'm going to write to all of them."

I wrote letters to all twenty-six people. I said, "I want to write this letter to you because I felt hindered in my personal growth when you did X, Y or Z. I know you did not mean to hurt me, and you didn't wake up in the morning saying, "I'm going to go hurt Jim"; but your actions did hurt me, and I want you to know that I completely forgive you. I want to release you from any bad effects of that. And I also want to tell you that I pray you will grow in God and be blessed by Him with his grace, mercy, and peace."

When I was deciding which one to send, I knew I didn't need to send any of them! My surprising realization was that God had made me bigger in my heart than all these twenty-six people and the things they had done to hinder me. I felt amazing freedom, and I still feel that freedom today, many years later. How about you try it?

> You have caused men to ride over our heads; We went through fire and through water; But You brought us out to rich fulfillment. (Psalm 66:12)
>
> I would have lost heart, unless I had believed that I would see the goodness of the LORD in the land of the living. Wait on the LORD; Be of good courage, and He shall strengthen your heart; Wait, I say, on the LORD! (Psalm 27:13–14)
>
> Therefore, having been justified by faith, we have peace with God through our Lord Jesus Christ, through whom also we have access by faith into this grace in which we stand, and rejoice in hope of the glory of God. And not only that, but we also glory in tribulations, knowing that tribulation produces perseverance; and perseverance, character; and character, hope. (Romans 5:1–4)

Your painful or confusing experiences are your enrollment in God's school of personal growth. He is invested in you, and He will see you through.

STEPS TO REINTERPRETING A LOSS

Take a moment to pause and consider your own life. Can you admit that it is dangerous to drift away from God? Can you remember a time when you began to cool off in your attitude toward God or toward your church life? Have you blamed God or others for a loss of money or a loved one? When was the last time you got mad at God? Are you still mad, or have you resolved that? Can you see the good that has come out of bad situations in your past? How would you help someone who is going through the same trial that you have gone through? Would you point them to a biblical example or a promise from God that covers their problem? If you notice you are stuck, what is your next step?

This chapter is here to help you look at the disappointment of the loss and turn it back into a productive tool. Reinterpreting some of your most difficult experiences involves the following steps.

First, identify your big loss. Then, compare your situation to a similar one in the Bible or to that of someone who overcame it. For example, you might have an acquaintance who experienced the loss of a large amount of money, a relationship, or a child, and they came through it. There is always someone else who has had the same problem as you. If you can talk with that person, do! Read their story if they have published it. If you find a Bible example, study that story.

There is always someone else who has had the same problem as you. If you can talk with that person, do!

Second, look at the facts in the case. What was it about? Find your underlying reasons, feelings, and priorities in the event. How did you interpret its meaning?

Third and most importantly, ask God what He is trying to accomplish in you through this event. You can then change your response to match the Lord's viewpoint about it. "And we know that all things work together for good to those who love God, to those who are the called according to His purpose" (Romans 8:28).

If we reexamine our response to a big loss or a trial, often we can find some chain that we held onto. When we kept an improper interpretation of the event, as one of the Old Testament prophets called it, we made "a covenant with death." This is signaled when we use the word "never." For example:

"I'll never trust men again."

"Never ask me to serve in church."

"I won't launch out again, so I will never fail like that again."

Our Messiah came to proclaim liberty to the captives. And now, if we want to be free to grow in Christ, we must look at those events again, look at our interpretation of them, and let God clean up those interpretations and explain His goodness in those events. Beth had to let go of the idea that being busy in church was the answer to everything, and I had to let go of the idea that God was going to automatically bring money flowing in from anything I did. Both Dolores and I had to quit blaming others for our identity in God or lack of growth. And I had to forgive others and take responsibility for my own life in God. It's so very important to see how loss can be a tool for growth. According to 2 Corinthians 4:17, "our light affliction, which is but for a moment, is working for us a far more exceeding and eternal weight of glory."

AN INVITATION

Do you resonate with any of the stories here? Did you realize that you plateaued or lost your edge somewhere along the way?

I invite you to share your own story of your trial or loss, how it affected you or still affects you or a loved one, and how you responded. Send that story to me on my website www.newcovenantlife.com. I welcome in-progress stories, and I want to hear from you.

The next chapter tells how asking "who" instead of "how" completely changed my life. Get ready, because I'm going to show you its power!

"I will restore to you the years that the swarming locust has eaten."

— Joel 2:25

Section Two

WHAT DO I NEED TO KNOW?

CHAPTER 4

It's All About Switching from How-To to Who-To

Discovering Rest in Christ

In the 1970s I lived in Lake Havasu City, a desert town in Arizona. Scorpions, rattlesnakes, lizards, and roadrunners had lived there for thousands of years. It was really their home, but humans had recently begun to move in. It was almost always hot and over 120ºF at times. As a postal service clerk, I was sorting mail one summer day in a little cubbyhole building made from bricks, mailboxes, and a steel door. It had a small air conditioner that I appreciated very much in this season. I had no inkling this would be the most life-changing day in my entire Christian experience.

Suddenly I heard a voice in my mind — a voice I recognized as God's.

"You like to study the Bible, don't you?"

"Yes," I replied.

"You have studied the doctrine of Scripture."

"Yes."

"You have studied the doctrine of Christ."

"Yes."

"You studied the doctrine of sin, redemption, and the church."

"Yes."

I was feeling very good about myself, hearing that God liked my studying. Then the unexpected came. "It seems to Me you want to know everything about the Bible so you won't need Me to live." I felt like He had opened the door, shot an arrow through my soul, then quickly run out.

Ouch! When I heard that, I said, "I am so sorry, Lord. I didn't realize I'd been dishonoring You. I've been trusting my own knowledge to please You. You wanted something better than that, something more relational, more intimate. I'm thankful that You are willing to address this blind spot in my life."

He was speaking according to John 5:39–40, where Jesus said, "You search the Scriptures, for in them you think you have eternal life; and these are they which testify of Me. But you're not willing to come to Me that you may have life." This statement by Jesus is the core truth we desperately need. "We know that we all have knowledge. Knowledge puffs up, but love edifies." (1 Corinthians 8:1).

THE GALATIAN TRAP

I spent almost twenty plateaued years working hard to be a good Christian without much progress. When I first met Jesus as my Savior, I was sure of heaven, but I followed up with years of working hard in my own power. Like the Galatians, I began in the Spirit, but now I was trying to be made mature in the flesh. Here is how the Apostle Paul put it:

O foolish Galatians! Who has bewitched you that you should not obey the truth, before whose eyes Jesus Christ was clearly portrayed among you as crucified? This only I want to learn from you: Did you receive the Spirit by the works of the law, or by the hearing of faith? Are you so foolish? Having begun in the Spirit, are you now being made perfect by the flesh? Have you suffered so many things in vain — if indeed it was in vain? Therefore, He who supplies the Spirit to you and works miracles among you, does He do it by the works of the law, or by the hearing of faith? (Galatians 3:1–5)

Most of us have done this. My Christian life was supported by the general thinking and preaching available during those days. I often heard a sermon that I could characterize in a four-point outline somewhat like this:

1. You're not doing enough praying, giving, reading, or whatever.
2. Try harder to do more of it. Make a commitment. Just say no to selfishness.
3. We will pray for you before you go home so that you can get victory.
4. Come back next week for more of the same.

I listened to many sermons like this, and I liked them. It's no wonder I worked hard for years to try to be a very good Christian and had often failed. Caught in the Galatian trap by trying to be perfected by the flesh, I was "powered by Jim" and not by the Holy Spirit and Jesus Christ! This dependence on the human power of self, weekly recommitments, and trying harder always leads to a plateaued life. God, in His grace, brought me to Himself to bring love and freedom in Christ.

TURNING POINTS IN FLAGSTAFF

"And let him who thirsts come. Whoever desires, let him take the water of life freely" (Revelation 22:17). God began to impress on me that I could have all of Him that I wanted. I remember driving around Flagstaff, Arizona, and being at the stop sign at Fourth Street and Route 66. I wanted to jump out of my car and tell everybody, "Hey, you can have all of God that you want!" I was just in awe at the thought, the reality, the truth that I can have all of God I want. As I thought about it over quite a long time, it just rolled around in my soul and flushed out all my doubts. God gives His children all of Himself. I want it. It's a *deal*!

When I was driving past a farmer's big field in Flagstaff, I caught myself saying, "Wow, if I had a hundred acres, what could I do with it? I could give more money to the church and missions." I realized I was using my income level as an excuse. I began thinking of the gift of time God has given. I have the same twenty-four hours every day that the apostles Peter and Paul did. What could I do with those twenty-four hours each day? Could I accomplish more with my life like they did?

Then I considered how my bills hindered me and how my children were a lot of work, and I blamed my church and my level of debt. What if my spouse won't change? I realized upon reflection that even if no one else changes, I can be sure that I will change. How many people and circumstances I mistakenly blamed for hindering my spiritual growth! It was time for me to learn the lesson: you do not have to wait for anyone in your life to change before you can draw nearer to God. I was thrilled and began seeking God with a renewed vigor and vision.

Who or what might you be blaming for hindering your spiritual life? Note any source outside yourself that you're secretly blaming for your stagnant Christian life. Is it a spouse? Or the amount of debt you have, your boss, your city, your fam-

> *You do not have to wait for anyone in your life to change before you can draw nearer to God.*

ily, or your church? Are you willing to let that go right now and ask Jesus to release you from the excuses you trusted? You can change! Even when no one else changes, don't wait; focus on the one in the mirror! Your prayer: "My Father, forgive me for blaming anyone else for my own failings. Please work your pleasure in me."

ASKING GOD TO FIX ME OR REFER ME OUT

Over time I developed a deep desire to be free from besetting sins and to know God better. Continual failure increasingly disquieted me. I was so frustrated I considered leaving Christianity completely. I came to the place where I cried out, "God, if you can't or won't free me from sin, then please refer me out to someone who will. I'll go to Buddha, Krishna, meditation, yoga, anything! I'm serious. I'll move to another state, listen to any preacher, read any book, move my family, whatever." I sensed His answer: "I don't need to send you to someone else, but it will take some work for Me to do this in you." I said, "Okay, let's go!"

I began asking in earnest, why does Romans chapter 6 say in twelve different ways that we are dead to sin, freed from sin, alive to God, etc.? I didn't get it. I was not experiencing it. Another Scripture was hopeful: "And she will bring forth a Son, and you shall call His name JESUS, for He will save His people from their sins" (Matthew 1:21). The name Jesus means Savior. I wanted to know about this promise too. Does Jesus really save me from my sins in this life, or does He just save me from sin's eternal consequences? His answer came in ways I did not expect.

HIS SURPRISE ANSWER TO MY REQUEST FOR REST

I had another experience that meant more to me than I would ever have guessed. With five kids and a modest income, I was very busy working two jobs. I'd work an eight-to-five job Monday through Friday and throw newspapers every night from 2 a.m. to 5 a.m. I was paying car insurance for four cars — life was just tough, and I became weak. Sickness was unusual for me, but I was busy with youth sports, church, and overwhelmed with all the daily things of life. I became bedridden with an infection, and I missed a week of work.

From my sick bed, I said, "God, I need financial rest and rest from my busy time." To my surprise, I heard Him speak to me right away. "I'll give you rest financially. I'll give you rest from your busy time. And I'm going to give you spiritual rest also, and the spiritual rest will be the very best." My reaction to that was, "I have no idea what spiritual rest is, but go ahead, Lord. If You want to give it to me, I'll receive it." The answer to my sin problem and my busy problem began to unfold as He taught me about spiritual rest. He began with the concept of leaving how-to for who-to.

THE FAILURE OF HOW-TO VS. THE VICTORY OF WHO-TO

When God spoke to me in the desert cubbyhole, He indicated that knowledge of the Bible was not enough for life, but He wanted a continual reliance upon His power and person. Talking to Him about everything became more normal for me. I am still moved by God's words to me in the desert.

Notice in the table the different approaches to handling challenges. How-to leaves Him out of the conversation. We fail because we trust in our own power. Who-to leads to a lifestyle of talking with God about everything.

HOW-TO	WHO-TO
• I must first understand.	• I must first talk to my Lord Jesus.
• I use my intellect first, then pray.	• I talk with Him first, then plan.
• I employ my personal capabilities with the help of friends, organizations, and the internet.	• He empowers me in my inner man while He works all things together for good.
• I check with YouTube, podcasts, AI, and self-help books.	• I read His Word to encounter His wisdom.
• Other people give me advice.	• The Holy Spirit speaks to me, sometimes using people.
• I mostly fail.	• I experience His help.
• I have a Tree of Knowledge experience.	• I have a Tree of Life experience.

THE ROMANS CHAPTER 7 DILEMMA

The move from how-to to who-to is well-pictured by the frustration described by the Apostle Paul in Romans chapter 7, where he tries by human effort to obey the law and be free from sin. The law of sin and death always wins because in our flesh there is no good thing. Even though the law is good, our fleshly efforts to use it are powerless. In verse 24, Paul writes: "O wretched man that I am! Who will deliver me from this body of death?"

Have you at some frustration point asked, "How can I get victory over sin?" Have you bought books and searched podcasts and sermons to discover how to win? Did you redouble your efforts and prayers? Did you fail again? If so, then you know the vexation Paul also found.

But in Romans 7:24, Paul did not ask "*How* can I be free?" but "*Who* will free me?" Then he supplied the answer to this dilemma: "I thank God — through Jesus Christ our Lord!" (Romans 7:25). Paul goes on to rejoice in the victory Christ Jesus gives: "For the law of the Spirit of life in Christ Jesus has made me free from the law of sin and death" (Romans 8:2). I began asking in prayer, "What is this law of the Spirit of life in Christ Jesus?" Our Lord began to show me that entering rest in Christ would free me from my how-to failures. Andrew Murray gives the best explanation of Romans chapter 7 I have found. I highly recommend reading it in chapter 6 of his book *Absolute Surrender*.[5]

Those who quit trusting their human efforts and start to trust the living Christ Jesus begin to know God's spiritual rest. Everyone can find this rest. Finding deliverance from busyness and sin is *not* a how-to-do list of new habits, resolutions, and commitments to change. It's about making the move from how-to to who-to. Both the Old Testament and the New Testament witness to this. The Old Testament speaks of the law and how to be holy. The New Testament speaks more of who will make you holy and give you abundant life.

I was created in the image of and by a Who, not a how-to. That's why my life transformation was to depend on a Who, and to become a who that I wasn't before. I did not become a how-to, but I became a who.

Moving deeper into who-to with Christ follows the same steps by which you came to Him as Savior in the first place. It is still the "hearing of faith" (Romans 10) that takes your relationship with Him to the next level. If you don't make this

> *I was created in the image of and by a Who, not a how-to. That's why my life transformation was to depend on a Who, and to become a who that I wasn't before. I did not become a how-to, but I became a who.*

move closer to Him, you are certain to stay on the self-effort plateau. As you practice turning to your Savior for wisdom and answers, you will notice a change in your entire attitude. Fears will melt away. You will develop the confidence that He is working with you in all issues of life.

The phrase "from how-to to who-to" captures the central message of this book. The next chapter will show how this shift opens the door to hearing the voice of your Good Shepherd.

> *"And this is eternal life, that they may know You, the only true God, and Jesus Christ whom You have sent."*
>
> *— John 17:3*

CHAPTER 5

God Speaks, and You Can Hear Him

Learning to Have a Conversation with God

Remember the cubbyhole story that I told you a little earlier? God confronted me there: "You want to know everything about the Bible, so you don't need Me." I learned to depend on knowing Him and hearing from Him, not relying on my human-powered knowledge about Him.

I heard God clearly another time, and it was easy to recognize His voice. A few decades ago, I worked with a woman ("Judy") who bothered me a lot. I had finally just had it and brought the situation to God. I said, "This person bothers me a lot! What do you want me to do about this?" I heard Him reply in my mind: "I'm going to give you four choices. Love her. Bless her. Do good to her. Pray for her." He was repeating His words from Matthew 5:44, and this made it easy to hear Him clearly. God knew just how to get right to the point.

He was pointing at my heart and attitude, so I determined to bless Judy.

We started our workday at about 4:00 a.m., and I decided to bring donuts in once a week and make sure she got one. I would always say, "Judy, I want to make sure you get a donut." She had gotten under my skin with her attitude, but after I started bringing her donuts, something happened in me. I don't know if anything happened in her, but she became one of my best friends at work, and I was truly sad when she moved away a few years later. God is so wise! We are designed to hear from Him, and when we do, and it agrees with His Word, it's always something we can act on.

God wants connection with us that is carried out in the context of conversation. You hear Him, and He hears you. He built the ability to have this communication inside you when you were created in His image. If Adam and Eve talked with Him, how much more may we expect to now that Christ has restored our relationship with God? When was the last time you expected to hear from God?

GOD CALLS US BY FAMILY NAMES

God calls us His friends, sons, daughters, ambassadors, and children. And in many ways, the New Testament shows that God doesn't want to just put a bunch of rules on the wall and have us try to follow them. That would make us feel that He is far away from us. Rather, He wants to live inside us. "As God has said: 'I will dwell in them and walk among them. I will be their God, and they shall be My people'" (2 Corinthians 6:16).

The picture that God has for us is called fellowship and partnership, and it's a relationship that God wants. It is significant that when Jesus listed the two great commandments,

He said the first is relation with God, and the second is relations with people (Mark 12:30–31). Let us pay attention to the depth of this.

WHAT INTIMACY WITH GOD LOOKS LIKE

When a young man starts talking with a young woman, they first talk about surface stuff — where they live, how old they are, and those sorts of things. The first level of conversation is just information, but then hopefully, as they go on, a deeper sharing happens. The couple must go deeper or break up. The hope is to find somebody with whom you may share very intimately and then trust enough to marry.

In the same way, in our relationship with God, if we only know facts about Him and His Son, we've not yet progressed to where He wants us to go. The ability to quote the Lord's Prayer, Bible verses, or even some of the confessions of the faith does not constitute knowing God since it is only knowing *about* God.

Jesus talked to us about this, and I'll repeat again what He said in John 5:39–40: "You search the Scriptures, for in them you think you have eternal life… But you are not willing to come to Me that you may have life." He's protesting that just intellectually knowing Him is not enough. We all probably know someone who has a lot of knowledge of the Bible, but they don't seem to really know Jesus or act like Him. That's not where we want to be. It's very sad when communion with God, who is called Love, is replaced with information about God or activity for God, and no intimacy develops. God "… also made us sufficient as ministers of the new covenant, not of the letter but of the Spirit; for the letter kills, but the Spirit gives life" (2 Corinthians 3:6). We don't live by "the letter," or knowledge or rules; our real life is from the Spirit and communion with God.

How do we measure closeness with others?

1. Frequency of communication
2. Depth of self-revelation
3. Sharing of goals, dreams, and opinions

These are good areas to use to assess your own relationship with God. How often do you address God throughout your day? Do you acknowledge Him when you wake up: "God, thank you for another day!" When you're wondering what to do in a situation, do you find yourself asking, "God, what do You know about this? What should I do?" You can even notice His Spirit nudging you to talk with someone or to avoid an event. Have you poured out your desires to God about your marriage or your kids or your future? Have you shared with Him how you feel about a weakness you struggle with or a strength you want to use effectively? Have you heard or felt God's heart toward His children? You can invite God to show you more of Himself, and He will oblige. One way He might do this is to suddenly give you an all-inclusive picture of one of His aspects — like His love as an ocean that fills the universe. You can tell God about your dreams and goals, then recognize Him telling you about His dreams and goals.

GOD HAS ALWAYS TALKED WITH MEN

Since the beginning in the garden with Adam and Eve, God spoke to them even when they wouldn't talk to Him. He went looking for Adam, saying, "Adam, where are you?" He wanted to talk to them. God is still the same. Are you aware that He wants to talk to you? God also had a conversation with Cain when Cain was angry that God was trying to help him overcome sin in Genesis 4:6–7. Do you ever feel you are too sinful for Him to talk to you? Take heart; Cain had perhaps a longer conversation than many people have had with Him. God talked with Moses and the prophet Samuel, and when He talked, it was so good that they wrote it down.

God says things about false gods like: "I talk, but they don't; they have mouths, but they don't speak. They have ears and they don't hear. They have hands, but they don't do anything, and they have feet, but they don't walk." He highlights that He is different from them because He does speak to men. See Psalm 115:4–8 and Psalm 135:15–18.

There is evidence for this in the Book of Genesis, during Israel's wandering in the wilderness after leaving Egypt, during David's time, and after that. "For I did not speak to your fathers, or command them in the day that I brought them out of the land of Egypt, concerning burnt offerings or sacrifices. But this is what I commanded them, saying, 'Obey My voice, and I will be your God, and you shall be My people'" (Jeremiah 7:22–23).

About three hundred years after King David's reign, God spoke to His people who were about to go into captivity for their disobedience. "I spoke to you in your prosperity, but you said, 'I will not hear.' This has been your manner from your youth, that you did not obey My voice" (Jeremiah 22:21). In Psalm 95:7–8, written many years after the Israelites were in the wilderness, His voice is mentioned: "For He is our God, and we are the people of His pasture, and the sheep of His hand. Today, if you will hear His voice: 'Do not harden your hearts, as in the rebellion, as in the day of trial in the wilderness.'" Notice how plainly He pointed out *His voice*.

Observe when you read the Psalms, that David was very conversational with God. In Psalm 6, David is straight with God. Here's my paraphrase: "God, please don't correct me when You are angry and don't punish me when You are really mad;

remember me with mercy because I am weak." He talked regularly and familiarly to God, which I've always liked. When I was young, I read a book by Malcolm Boyd called *Are You Running with Me, Jesus?*[6] The prayers were very conversational, and I am still impressed by that.

In the New Testament, Jesus said He expects us to hear His voice.

If God spoke to His children in the Old Testament, why do we think He would speak less in the New Testament? We are still His beloved children, and He is still a speaking Father. A medical doctor in church told me he thought that only some people had a special gift of hearing God's voice. He thought this was like other gifts of healing, tongues, and preaching, which only belong to a few. This untruth kept him from hearing his Father's voice for many years. Don't let it rob *you*. Review the following statements of Jesus.

> And when he brings out his own sheep, he goes before them; and the sheep follow him, for they know his voice. Yet they will by no means follow a stranger, but will flee from him, for they do not know the voice of strangers. (John 10:4–5)
>
> I am the good shepherd; and I know My sheep, and am known by My own. As the Father knows Me, even so I know the Father; and I lay down My life for the sheep. And other sheep I have which are not of this fold; them also I must bring, and they will hear My voice; and there will be one flock and one shepherd. (John 10:14–16)
>
> My sheep hear My voice, and I know them, and they follow Me. (John 10:27)

He didn't say most disciples won't hear Him except special ones; He said all His sheep hear His voice.

He didn't say hearing Him would end when He left.

He didn't say hearing Him would end when the apostles died.

He simply said His sheep hear His voice, and they won't follow a stranger's voice. Sadly, some Christians speak like they believe the devil talks to them more than their Heavenly Father does! How sad is that? If you're not hearing God's voice, it's because somebody talked you out of it. And this is likely from the enemy himself or from people who are justifying why they don't hear His voice themselves. Don't let anyone tell you that you can't hear your Shepherd's voice. Don't we know something is wrong in a rela-

> *If you're not hearing God's voice, it's because somebody talked you out of it.*

tionship if regular two-way conversation is missing? Jesus expects to be talking to us constantly, and He expects us to be hearing Him. When tempted by the devil, Jesus said: "Man shall not live by bread alone, but by every word [proceeding] from the mouth of God" (Matthew 4:4). The word "proceeding" is represented as "that proceeds" in the New King James translation, but "proceeding" is a more accurate translation of the original Greek. The tense on the verb "proceeding" indicates it's constantly happening — God's word is always proceeding to His sons and daughters. It's wonderful to hear His voice, and I love hearing Him. I grew in this, and you can too!

Jesus said He would still speak to us through the Holy Spirit after His ascension.

In His farewell address in John chapters 14–16, Jesus said:

These things I have spoken to you while being present with you. But the Helper, the Holy Spirit, whom the Father will send in My name, He will teach you all things, and bring to your remembrance all things I have said to you. (John 14:25–26)

But when the Helper comes, whom I shall send to you from the Father, the Spirit of truth who proceeds from the Father, He will testify of Me. (John 15:26)

However, when He, the Spirit of truth, has come, He will guide you into all truth. (John 16:13)

To sum it up, *the Holy Spirit is the delivery person of God's voice.* When you are reminded of a Scripture verse, it is helpful to thank the Holy Spirit for reminding you of it, per John 14:26. Many times, when you hear what God is speaking to you, it is while reading the Bible.

> ***The Holy Spirit is the delivery person of God's voice.***

One memorable time I heard God was when my first wife was pregnant with our first child, and we moved into a larger apartment. My wife wanted to buy some towels to match the colors of the apartment bathroom, but when she did, I felt extremely uncomfortable. I felt like she was spending more money than we had, and because my soul was so troubled, I asked God about it. "What's going on here?" Very quickly, the Holy Spirit said, "You think she's like your stepmom because you used to ride to school with your dad, who would say every day, 'Jimmy, she's killing me. She wants me to buy a big fancy house, and she's going to spend all our money.'" When the Holy Spirit pointed out to me that I saw my wife as my stepmom, I realized that I was reliving a life story from my past. I was interpreting a simple request for towels as someone sending me into the poor house. My dad's passive self-pity was talking to me and trying to influence me.

God knew how to accurately arrest my thoughts and guide me into truth. I chose to reinterpret my wife's request and avoided going into fear of poverty or resentment toward my wife. God is so good!

It was normal in the book of Acts for the disciples to hear the Holy Spirit.

Church leaders heard the Holy Spirit very clearly.

> Now in the church that was at Antioch there were certain prophets and teachers… As they ministered to the Lord and fasted, the Holy Spirit said, "Now separate to Me Barnabas and Saul for the work to which I have called them." Then, having fasted and prayed, and laid hands on them, they sent them away. (Acts 13:1–3)

After the church had discussed whether Gentile Christian believers had to keep the law of Moses or not, they decided that they didn't need to. They wrote to the churches and included the Holy Spirit's leading: "For it seemed good to the Holy Spirit, and to us, to lay upon you no greater burden than these necessary things: that you abstain from things offered to idols, from blood, from things strangled, and from sexual immorality. If you keep yourselves from these, you will do well. Farewell" (Acts 15:28–29). See also Acts 16:6–10.

It continues to be normal to hear God's voice today.

Jesus said, "If anyone loves Me, he will keep My word; and My Father will love him, and We will come to him and make Our home with him" (John 14:23). If God comes and lives in you as His home, is He going to talk? Have you ever had a visitor come to your house and stay for a day, a week, or the rest of your life and never talk to you? It would be unthinkable. Begin to see your Father and Jesus, your Savior, as living in you and wanting to discuss your everyday issues.

FREQUENCY OF HEARING GOD'S VOICE

If you've never heard God's voice, start with a simple prayer like mine: "Jesus, this is Jimmy. I heard that You speak to Your sheep, Your children, and that they can know Your voice. Please talk to me in a way I can hear You. Thank You. I'm waiting."

I came to the place where I asked, "God, how often does the Bible say that I might hear Your voice?" Here's the answer I found: "Therefore, as the Holy Spirit says: 'Today, if you will hear His voice, do not harden your hearts as in the rebellion, in the day of trial in the wilderness'" (Hebrews 3:7-8). Because of this verse, I began to expect God to speak to me at least once a day. The condition is to not harden your heart. Now, I wasn't particular about what He said to me, whether it was "Hello," "I love you," or "You need to fix this or fix that." I just began to enjoy knowing that He would talk to me at least once a day about something.

When you are reading the Gospels, the Holy Spirit is reminding you of things Jesus said (John 14:26). At times, these words come alive to you in a new way. This is more than intellectual knowledge, and it is good to recognize this as a way God speaks to you even when you didn't hear a physical voice.

To increase your experience of hearing His voice, I recommend a book written by Brother Lawrence called *The Practice of the Presence of God*.[7] Several different publishers have printed this treasure. Brother Lawrence was a Carmelite brother who lived from 1614 to 1691 and was a cook and a dishwasher in an abbey after he was injured in the Thirty Years' War. He was looking at a life of cooking and washing dishes in an abbey for the rest of his days, but he had a desire to talk to God and to hear from God. He learned to commune with God constantly even through his busy and humble life. This book will encourage you to experience the same.

After knowing it's possible and normal, one of the most useful keys to hearing from God is to be ready in attitude. When you pray, get alone and talk to your Father, who sees in secret, and He will reward you. The quiet alone time helps you focus on Him. My friend Dan says he asks God about a hundred questions a day. Start making it a normal part of your day to speak to God and ask Him questions. He will meet you!

"I learned from Hebrews 3:7–8 that the Holy Spirit speaks to me every day."

— Jim Kaminski

CHAPTER 6

You Must Picture Your Promised Land

Fulfilling God's Calling Before You Leave Earth

Nicholas was a 76-year-old Jewish man when he received Jesus as his Savior. Afterward I met him weekly to study the Bible. He asked, "Why don't Christians all commit suicide and just get on to heaven?" Apparently, he had heard that becoming a Christian consisted of being sure of going to heaven and then waiting until you die. This thought misses the calling and vision God has provided for you to fulfill while you are here. Your promised land is the life of fruitfulness, intimacy, and impact God wants you to live right now — not just someday in heaven.

> *Your promised land is the life of fruitfulness, intimacy, and impact God wants you to live right now — not just someday in heaven.*

YOUR PROMISED LAND ON EARTH

It would be a mistake to think that our Beloved Savior only waits for us at the end of the road. Would God start you on a Christian life and not be the Author and Finisher of your faith? What would the promised land look like for you, not in heaven, but here, during your time on earth?

Romans chapter 6 speaks of living free from sin, and the Apostle Paul urges us to live as Christ lived, and yet we're not doing it. I read about many conversions, miraculous healings, and powerful gifts of the Holy Spirit. "Ask what you will, and it will be done" (John 15:7, paraphrased). That wasn't me. I was frustrated when I compared my Christian life with what I read in the Bible. If your experience is like mine was, you're having an Old Covenant experience as a Christian, while living under the New Covenant Jesus set up. This creates great confusion in our minds. The Holy Spirit graciously brought me into the New Covenant life. In this chapter, we will see what we need to begin to do about it.

The promised land for you and me is generally that life, that promise, that sense you get from the Bible of a life you would love to have. For me, it would be a Christlike life, answered prayers, good family and church experience, Holy Spirit gifts, and to live as a blessing like God promised to Abraham (Genesis 12:1–3).

Why do I ask what the promised land is for you and tell you to picture it? I do it because you have inherited Abraham's blessing (Galatians 3:9,14). You also have a beautiful vision that God put in your heart. It might be meaningful work, peaceful family life, a Christian ministry, salvation of loved ones, or other blessings. Scripture invites us to visualize it. You wouldn't think of moving to a new city or picking a new home without first walking it and looking it over. Now look at your promised land and walk through it in your mind's eye. He promises to give it to you! Don't let anyone talk you out of it. What is your heart crying out for?

We can look to the stories of Abraham, Moses, Joshua, Jeremiah, Ezekiel, and Jesus for more information about this.

ABRAHAM: SEEING AND WALKING THE PROMISE

Abraham's story is one of blessing:

> And the LORD said to Abram, after Lot had separated from him: "Lift your eyes now and look from the place where you are — northward, southward, eastward, and westward; for all the land which you see I give to you and your descendants forever. And I will make your descendants as the dust of the earth; so that if a man could number the dust of the earth, then your descendants also could be numbered. Arise, walk in the land through its length and its width, for I give it to you. (Genesis 13:14–17)

Abraham's message: God has promised and will give us a fruitful life. "And in you all the families of the earth shall be blessed" (Genesis 12:3). You are called to live and fulfill the promise of blessing many people. God told Abraham to walk the land He showed him. We must also. Is there a promise God has shown you that you're afraid to walk into?

MOSES: THE FRUSTRATION OF SELF-EFFORT

Moses was headed to the Promised Land after forty years of wandering the desert with a difficult group of people. When it was almost time to go into the Promised Land, he had this conversation with God:

> Then I pleaded with the LORD at that time, saying: "... I pray, let me cross over and see the good land beyond the Jordan, those pleasant mountains, and Lebanon." But the LORD was angry with me on your account, and would not listen to me. So the LORD said to me: "Enough of that! Speak no more to Me of this matter. Go up to the top of Pisgah, and lift your eyes toward the west, the north, the south, and the east; behold it with your eyes, for you shall not cross over this Jordan. But command Joshua, and encourage him and strengthen him; for he shall go over before this people, and he shall cause them to inherit the land which you will see." (Deuteronomy 3:23, 25–28)

Moses deeply wanted the Promised Land. He had written the laws and rules for living there. He knew it flowed with milk and honey. He begged three times, but God said he couldn't enter it but only see it. Understand that Moses can help you see your promised land, but he can't take you in.

The Moses kind of life is characterized by motivation coming from good laws and external rules while you lack heart obedience. You are trying hard in your own power to improve but still failing too much and living an up-and-down Christian life. Sadly, many Christian leaders have told us this is the normal experience. If we are trying to earn our promised land, we are a New Testament person living an Old Testament life. Moses's failure to enter is the picture of our trying hard under our own power to gain our promised land.

Moses's message became: I can show you how wonderful the Promised Land looks, I can stir up your desire for it, but I can't take you in. But if Moses symbolizes the limits of living by laws (the how-to life), what — or who — leads us forward? You must follow your Joshua, and He will cause you to inherit it.

Moses's failure to enter is the picture of our trying hard under our own power to gain our promised land.

JOSHUA: ENTERING THROUGH CHRIST

After all his years of leadership, Moses was told to defer to Joshua. "But command Joshua, and encourage him and strengthen him; for he shall go over before this people, and he shall cause them to inherit the land which you will see" (Deuteronomy 3:28).

And God told Joshua, "Every place that the sole of your foot will tread upon I have given you, as I said to Moses... Be strong and of good courage, for to this people you shall divide as inheritance the land which I swore to their fathers to give them" (Joshua 1:3,6).

Joshua's message: Joshua is symbolic of Jesus in the New Testament — even the names are the same. The Greek name of Jesus is generally understood to be a transliteration of the Hebrew name Joshua. Jesus is commissioned to *cause* God's people to enter their promised land. He is the Author and Finisher of our faith. Though Moses and living by laws will stir your desire to go, only Jesus can take you in. Joshua is the picture of Christ leading God's people and

Jesus is commissioned to cause God's people to enter their promised land.

causing them to inherit it. It's His power that causes us to inherit our promised land and its blessings. Are you living under Moses, "how-to," or walking with Joshua (Jesus), "who-to"?

When your vision aligns with God's promises, and you start to expect from Him, your life can change. Take time to write down your vision of a promised land life. You might envision living waters flowing from within you and victory over your enemies as God leads you from strength to strength. Or you might see God as your always-present friend and protector. You can envision being free from fear and doubt. You can imagine healing and provision or leading many to Christ. Write down your own hopes, dreams, and plans to help you.

Remember, this New Covenant life was made possible by Jesus and is also powered by His Holy Spirit. It's not all up to you. "Do not fear, little flock, for it is your Father's good pleasure to give you the kingdom" (Luke 12:32).

"Joshua (Jesus) will cause God's people to inherit the land that Moses will only see."

— **Paraphrase of Deuteronomy 3:28**

CHAPTER 7

You Can Live the Promised New Covenant

Accepting a New Heart and a Fruitful Life

After fifteen years of studying and working hard to grow in Christ, I realized I had plateaued in my experience. What did that look like? I received few answers to my prayers and saw no miracles at home or in church. I did not sense in me the overflowing love for people that Jesus described, and I still focused on trying to convince others that my doctrine was right. I was frustrated trying to tell my loved ones that I knew what God wanted *them* to do. Others who were clearly in love with Jesus struck me as odd people who had some secret I could not discover.

Where were the miracles and mighty signs I was reading about? Why didn't revival come to our church? I dreamed of a great church experience like I had read about in the book of Acts. Where was it? Was God withholding it according to some big plan He had? Was I not worthy of His favor? I thought

"Where is the God of Elijah?" as I read stories of great moves of God in the last few centuries.

As a believer, I understood that God would receive me into heaven when I died someday, but until then, I needed to work hard at being the best Christian I could be. Was I also following the way of Moses and the law? Why didn't I have life in myself to naturally follow my Wonderful Savior?

Have you ever felt disappointed because your Christian life seemed like Israel's up-and-down history in the Old Testament? They were repeatedly backsliding into idolatry and disobedience. The people's hearts were not steadfast with God, and reformations lasted a short time then fizzled out when the leader changed. Do you lose zeal soon after a revival at your church?

Israel's Old Testament historical books of Joshua, Judges, Samuel, and Kings describe the people doing well under a good leader, like King David, but always backsliding into idolatry after he died. They could not thrive under an evil king like Ahab. Have you thrived under a good pastor only to flop when he was replaced?

Since Moses himself could not enter the Promised Land, it is no surprise that the law he brought could not lead others into it. In some mysterious way, Moses, with his law, was transmitting through the centuries an inability to stay faithful. Sadly, this same failure is still lived out in our modern-day churches by too many people. Could it be because today we are still living under law?

Many Christians struggle not because they lack sincerity, but because they try to live the Christian life with Old Covenant methods. The Old Covenant life is comprised of attitudes, beliefs,

Many Christians struggle not because they lack sincerity, but because they try to live the Christian life with Old Covenant methods.

and lifestyles based on works and "how-to." You are living the old way if you are:

- Trusting your own power to change and improve while you try to obey rules and laws that are not in your heart (chapter 4)
- Not hearing your Shepherd's voice daily because you believe you can't, and you prefer that your leader talk for God instead (chapter 5)
- Only seeking your own safety because you lack interest or vision to live fruitfully by abiding in Jesus (chapter 6)
- Not trusting that the Holy Spirit is continually forming you into the image of God's Son (chapter 6)
- Burnt out from living the how-to life based on works (chapter 4)

As I said in the previous chapter, it's a mistake to think that our Beloved only waits for us at the end of the path. Knowing the strength needed for the journey, would our Heavenly Father start us off then send us out alone and wish us good luck? No! Because the law could not give life, God sent His Son to be our Life! Up to this time, no one had told me that my Savior lived inside me to give me life. But one day someone led me to study the promised New Covenant. What a blessed day!

God saw that Israel did not cooperate with His desire to dwell among them, to make them kings and priests, and to bless all the families of the earth through them. This is why God promised to bring in a New Covenant that would remedy all the faults of the Old Covenant of the law of Moses. God designed it to give His people a new heart, His law in our minds, and the Savior living inside each child of God. He sent His Son Jesus to bring in the promised New Covenant. He chose the prophets Jeremiah and Ezekiel to reveal the New Covenant life.

THE NEW COVENANT IN JEREMIAH

God told Jeremiah what He was planning to do — how thoroughly He was going to provide for a new kind of life in His child.

> Behold, the days are coming, says the Lord, when I will make a new covenant with the house of Israel and with the house of Judah — not according to the covenant that I made with their fathers in the day that I took them by the hand to lead them out of the land of Egypt, My covenant which they broke, though I was a husband to them, says the LORD. But this is the covenant that I will make with the house of Israel after those days, says the LORD: I will put My law in their minds, and write it on their hearts; and I will be their God, and they shall be My people. No more shall every man teach his neighbor, and every man his brother, saying, "Know the LORD," for they all shall know Me, from the least of them to the greatest of them, says the LORD. For I will forgive their iniquity, and their sin I will remember no more."
> (Jeremiah 31:31–34)

When He said, "I will put My law in their minds, and write it on their hearts," God made it an inside salvation. That is why you suddenly care about God's will after you receive Christ as Savior. He has moved inside your heart, and you have a new awareness that your life is about Him and what He wants.

"And I will make an everlasting covenant with them, that I will not turn away from doing them good; but I will put My fear in their hearts so that they will not depart from Me" (Jeremiah 32:40). Try to understand how great this New Covenant promise is. We need Him to put His fear and reverence in us to ensure we will not leave Him by backsliding or plateauing.

THE NEW COVENANT IN EZEKIEL

Ezekiel, like Jeremiah, also foresaw this radical transformation:

> I will give you a new heart and put a new spirit within you; I will take the heart of stone out of your flesh and give you a heart of flesh. I will put My Spirit within you and cause you to walk in My statutes, and you will keep My judgments and do them. (Ezekiel 36:26–27)

There is no such thing as a Christian believer who has an evil heart since Christ has replaced it with a new heart indwelt by His Spirit. Only our Lord is powerful enough to promise these things and to make them true in us. Jesus said, "The things which are impossible with men are possible with God" (Luke 18:27). We now live in the "who" ... Jesus!

THE NEW COVENANT AND THE LAST SUPPER

Jesus instituted the New Covenant at the Last Supper, and it is in force today. "Likewise He also took the cup after supper, saying, 'This cup is the new covenant in My blood, which is shed for you'" (Luke 22:20). Jesus proclaimed that He was bringing us into the New Covenant relationship with the

Father. He has now taken His place as the Joshua who causes us to inherit our promised land. Take a moment to realize how big this is — that entering in is not dependent on your ability, but on His.

Vine and branches show a New Testament promised land.

The best picture of your promised land in this life on earth in the New Testament is in John 15.

> I am the true vine, and My Father is the vine-dresser. Every branch in Me that does not bear fruit He takes away; and every branch that bears fruit He prunes, that it may bear more fruit. You are already clean because of the word which I have spoken to you. Abide in Me, and I in you. As the branch cannot bear fruit of itself, unless it abides in the vine, neither can you, unless you abide in Me. I am the vine, you are the branches. He who abides in Me, and I in him, bears much fruit; for without Me you can do nothing. If anyone does not abide in Me, he is cast out as a branch and is withered; and they gather them and throw them into the fire, and they are burned. If you abide in Me, and My words abide in you, you will ask what you desire, and it shall be done for you. By this My Father is glorified, that you bear much fruit; so you will be My disciples. (John 15:1–8)
>
> These things I command you, that you love one another. (John 15:17)

Jesus says that being His branches, we are clean. What we do now is:

- Glorify the Father – the Vision
- Bear fruit – the Activity
- Abide in Him, "who-to" – the Power
- Love one another – the Daily Experience

There is no hint here of staying safe, of waiting to die to go to heaven, or of not giving the Father a return on His investment in us. Notice that glorifying Father God by fruitfulness is the great priority in the New Covenant. When Jesus commanded us to love one another, He also demonstrated that there is no life as sweet as living in service and love with one another. God makes it natural for us as branches to draw in life from the vine and put out fruit through ourselves.

> *God makes it natural for us as branches to draw in life from the vine and put out fruit through ourselves.*

TESTIMONY TO THE GREATNESS OF THE NEW COVENANT

In Hebrews 8:6–13, we read that the New Covenant is a better covenant, with better promises, is not faulty, and makes the first covenant obsolete. Remember Jesus said, "Do not think that I came to destroy the Law or the Prophets. I did not come to destroy but to fulfill" (Matthew 5:17). In instituting the New Covenant, Jesus first fulfilled the necessary requirements of Old Covenant law.

Let us ask, as Paul did in the epistle to the Galatians, what the law was designed to do. There he explains that the law was designed to be temporary as a tutor to bring us to Jesus (Galatians 3:17,19, 23–25). If the law was meant to be a temporary tutor and the Old Covenant a temporary experience, then why do Christians live an Old Covenant type of life? The answer is we haven't heard that Jesus is the One who brings us into the New Covenant, promised land life. The good news is that Jesus overcame the failures of Old Covenant life and provided a successful New Covenant life for you. Your promised land will be the one that *flows* with milk and honey, not the one that you have been pumping!

In the next chapter, we will look at the wonderful provision of the inside Christ who causes you to live a New Covenant life. You can pray now, "Jesus, I see you have given me a new heart. Thank You! Forgive me for believing the lie that I am shackled with an evil heart. Teach me afresh to trust You working in my New Covenant heart."

"He who abides in Me, and I in him, bears much fruit."

— *Jesus, in John 15:5*

There's More to Learn About the Inside Christ

Knowing Jesus Is the Way to Grow

"We'll hardly get our feet out of time into eternity that we'll bow our heads in shame and humiliation. We'll gaze on eternity and say, 'Look at all the riches there were in Jesus Christ, and I've come to the Judgment Seat almost a pauper.'"[8] This thought by A.W. Tozer haunted me. I had not yet learned that true spiritual growth does not come from outward effort or religious activity, but instead springs from intimately knowing Jesus as the indwelling Christ.

I began to realize I needed something different — I needed to somehow know Jesus more. After leading thousands of people to Christ, Charles Finney wrote, "... I hardly know in which of his many relations he appears most wonderful when in that relation he is revealed by the Holy Spirit."[9] I had thought I knew all about Christ, but happily, I found out I was very much mistaken. Christ's "many relations" to us? What? I had no idea what this meant, but as I began to seek to know Jesus better, my life started to change.

> *I had thought I knew all about Christ, but happily, I found out I was very much mistaken.*

JOHN THE BAPTIST WONDERED ABOUT JESUS TOO

John the Baptist seems to have asked the core question in Matthew 11:2–3. "And when John had heard in prison about the works of Christ, he sent two of his disciples and said to Him, 'Are You the Coming One, or do we look for another?'" Jesus answered John's disciples, instructing them to go tell John about the healing miracles they'd seen and the good news that was being preached to the poor.

John had heard of Jesus's many miracles, but it was a bleak time for him in prison. I found myself asking those same questions. Is Jesus the one who fixes everything? Is He the complete Savior who saves me from sin, does everything I need, answers my prayers, and performs miracles? Is He the One, or should I look for somebody else? I was looking for books, some mighty man of God, or the super church. I was looking for all sorts of things to help me, but not *Him*. With horror, I realized that I, too, was really looking for somebody besides Jesus! I repented of that and took courage in His promise in John 14:21: "And he who loves Me will be loved by My Father, and I will love him and manifest Myself to him." I began to pray this for myself: "Jesus, manifest Yourself to me. I need you."

SHE BELIEVED CHRIST WOULD TELL HER ALL THINGS

In John chapter 4, another person showed she had a larger hope than I did that the Messiah would do a complete job. Jesus guided the Samaritan woman at the well to review her checkered past, and He promised even so that she could have a fountain of living water streaming out of her. She said she wanted that living water! "The woman said to Him, 'I know that Messiah is coming' (who is called Christ). 'When He comes, He will tell us all things.' Jesus said to her, 'I who speak to you, am He'" (John 4:25–26).

From what this woman had heard about the coming Messiah, she understood that He would tell her everything she needed to hear. Couldn't I expect the same from the Savior? Didn't Jesus promise that the Holy Spirit will guide us into all truth (John 16:13)? When the Messiah comes, won't He tell me everything I really need for life? Why am I not hearing all these things?

We've tried many things: Bible studies, prayer, a different church, serving more, seminars, retreats, and even Google. But have we tried getting to know Jesus more? Did we ever think that this might be the key? I want to tell you that it is. It's a simple key.

Why have we tried everything except knowing Jesus more when the remedy for our problem is simply that? Following the Samaritan woman's lead, I began to trust Him to tell me everything I needed to hear. "What do I need to be closer to You, to get more answers to prayer, to hear from You more?" I began in childlike faith to ask Him all these questions. And I began to

> *We've tried many things: Bible studies, prayer, a different church, serving more, seminars, retreats, and even Google. But have we tried getting to know Jesus more?*

hear from Him in prayer and through Scriptures that the Holy Spirit made plain and meaningful to me.

Would you take a moment to pray this right now? "Jesus, You are my Messiah. You're everything that I need. Forgive me for seeking life in other things. Manifest yourself to me according to Your promise. Give me a drink of Your living water that will become a fountain of living water springing up to eternal life inside of me."

DO YOU HAVE THE INSIDE CHRIST?

Somehow, we have lost the idea that Jesus Christ now lives inside each believer who is a temple of the Holy Spirit. Andrew Murray well describes why in this quote:

> Let me say, in the first place, if you would know the power of this life: *Believe in and accept the indwelling Christ.* Let me ask you the question: Do you fully and truly believe in the indwelling Christ? You do believe in an incarnate Christ. When the name of Christ is mentioned, you at once think of One who was born a little babe at Bethlehem, who took our nature upon Him and lived as a man upon the earth. That thought is inseparable from your faith in Him. You believe, too, in the crucified Christ, dying on Calvary for our sins. You believe, too, in the risen Savior, one who lives for evermore. And you believe in the glorified Lord, now sitting on the throne of heaven. But do you believe as definitely — as naturally — in the indwelling Christ?[10]

Jesus plainly stated that He came to be an inside Christ. "A little while longer and the world will see Me no more, but you will see Me. Because I live, you will live also. At that day you will know that I am in My Father, and you in Me, and I in you" (John 14:19–20). This describes a salvation much better than we had hoped!

It's common to miss what Jesus is all about at first.

When we first become Christians, it's very common to not grasp just how critical the knowledge of Jesus is to our entire life. We know that we have passed from death to life and from unrighteousness to right standing with God. But the knowledge of Christ needed for initial salvation does not suffice for continued growth in Christ. It's normal for everyone to initially know Him but not realize how much more there is to know of Him. In this, we're in good company with the disciples and the Apostle Paul.

> *The knowledge of Christ needed for initial salvation does not suffice for continued growth in Christ.*

The disciples Thomas and Phillip

During Jesus's farewell address before the crucifixion, He said:

> And where I go you know, and the way you know. Thomas said to Him, "Lord, we do not know where You are going, and how can we know the way?" Jesus said to him, "I am the way, the truth, and the life. No one comes to the Father except through Me." Philip said to Him, "Lord, show

us the Father, and it is sufficient for us." Jesus said to him, "Have I been with you so long, and yet you have not known Me, Phillip? He who has seen Me has seen the Father; so how can you say, 'Show us the Father?'" (John 14:4-6, 8-9)

Peter and the Emmaus Road disciples

Even though the Father revealed to him that Jesus was the Christ, Peter still didn't understand Jesus when He washed his feet or when Peter denied Jesus three times. We can also read in Luke chapter 24 about the two disciples on the Emmaus Road who needed Jesus to enlighten them.

Peter's recommendation

I want you to notice a large emphasis on knowing Jesus and how important it is in the following passages. Jesus was Peter's earthly buddy for three years, and Peter knew Him a lot after being with Him that long. And yet after Jesus's resurrection and ascension, Peter said this: "but grow in grace and knowledge of our Lord and Savior Jesus Christ. To Him be the glory both now and forever. Amen" (2 Peter 3:18). There is so much about this glorious Jesus we need to keep discovering.

Peter again references this as the way to grow: "Grace and peace be multiplied through you in the knowledge of God and of Jesus our Lord, as His divine power has given to us all things that pertain to life and godliness, through the knowledge of Him who called us by glory and virtue" (2 Peter 1:2-3). How do we find everything we need for our lives? Through the knowledge of Him who called us by glory and virtue. Peter assures us that God *has* given us everything through the knowledge of Him. What did Peter know about growing in knowledge of

Jesus that we have missed? Let's find out in prayer and through Scripture as we welcome the Holy Spirit to expand our knowledge of Jesus.

I wanted to discover who Jesus is to me and who I am to Him. I knew I had to ask in prayer. I read the promise where Jesus said, "At that day you will know that I am in My Father, and you in Me, and I in you" (John 14:20). I began to pray that I would know that I am in Him and He is in me. I recommend this prayer to you.

Paul's experience

Beloved, there is so much more of Jesus. You will be amazed, and you will find yourself saying with Paul, "the unsearchable riches of Christ" (Ephesians 3:8).

> But what things were gain to me, these I have counted loss for Christ. Yet indeed I also count all things loss for the excellence of the knowledge of Christ Jesus my Lord, for whom I have suffered the loss of all things, and count them as rubbish, that I may gain Christ. (Philippians 3:7–8)

Paul didn't say he counted all his mistakes as rubbish. He said everything he thought was good about his religious life was rubbish compared to knowing Jesus.

PRAYERS TO KNOW JESUS MORE

From prison in his final days, Paul prayed with extreme desire: "that I may know Him and the power of His resurrection, and the fellowship of His sufferings, being conformed to His death, if, by any means, I may attain to the resurrection from the dead" (Philippians 3:10–11). Have you ever had enough boldness, courage, and desire to pray for these three things? That you would know the resurrected Christ, that you would know the fellowship of His suffering, and that you would be made more selfless and willing to die to the world and to sin. This is a very, very powerful prayer. If you don't think you're ready to pray this, if you're a little afraid about it, then ask God to help you.

Paul prayed another great prayer. Notice the emphasis on knowing Jesus:

> Therefore I also, after I heard of your faith in the Lord Jesus and your love for all the saints, do not cease to give thanks for you, making a mention of you in my prayers: that the God of our Lord Jesus Christ, the Father of glory, may give to you the spirit of wisdom and revelation in the knowledge of Him, the eyes of your understanding being enlightened; that you may know what is the hope of His calling, what are the riches of the glory of His inheritance in the saints, and what is the exceeding greatness of His power toward us who believe, according to the working of His mighty power which He worked in Christ when He raised Him from the dead and seated Him at His right hand in the heavenly places, far above all principality and power and might and dominion, and every name that is named, not only in this age but also in that which is to come. (Ephesians 1:15–21)

Paul demonstrates great emphasis on the importance of Jesus. You will know why when you seek to know Him more. He will not disappoint you.

The best book I know of to discover Jesus in His priestly relationships to us is *The Holiest of All*[11] by Andrew Murray. I encourage you to read that book and study through Hebrews. I found Jesus as my living Earthly High Priest, my living Heavenly High Priest, and the Mediator of the New Covenant. I have been mightily changed.

> *"My people are serving Me out of duty.*
> *I want them to serve Me out of love."*

> — **God, in a word to Jim Kaminski**

Section Three

WHAT DO I DO NOW?

CHAPTER 9

Let Jesus Bring It Out and Clean It Up

Saying Goodbye to Shame

I was reading a little devotional book written by Robert Boyd Munger called *My Heart–Christ's Home*.[12] In it he described Jesus coming to visit his home, which was really his life. As Jesus went into the different rooms of his life, Munger described his response to the presence of Jesus. As I read the book, I followed along with my own responses to Jesus visiting my house.

I let Jesus visit my study, representing the books I was reading and what I was feeding my mind — about which I was a little nervous. The next room Jesus went into was the dining room, which represented my appetites and desires for the things I deeply wanted. He also visited the rec room, which represented my entertainment life, what I watched on TV, and the sports I played.

The room that stood out most to me was the dirty closet in the hall. That's the hiding place where I threw stuff if we had surprise visitors. I would throw it in there, slam the door, and never open it for anyone to see even if they asked. "Jesus, I don't think you want to see in there." He looked at me with love in His eyes and said, "I already know what's in there, and I still love you." I said, "Really?" He said, "Yes, I do. I thoroughly know what's in there, and I love you anyway." That was disarming, but I was still very uncomfortable. I realized that I thought if people didn't know about my worst thoughts, attitudes, and actions, maybe God didn't. Or maybe I felt safe from people.

He said, "Let's open that closet, and I will help you clean it out." As I opened the door, we began to take things out. It was smelly, dirty, and very embarrassing. I realized He wasn't making me do it by myself; He was helping me do it! As we did it, I asked Him a question, "Why are You doing this painful thing to me?" He answered, "I don't want you to be ashamed." I was very touched and moved. I thanked Him for doing the painful closet-cleaning work with me.

WE LIVE FOR HIS EYES ONLY

I was shocked to catch myself wondering so often what people would think of me when I did something or said something. My concern about this was a big surprise for me, but I had to admit it was true that I cared what others thought. When we learn to live for God's eyes only, a big weight drops off our shoulders: the unbearable weight of what people will think. The only One whose opinion truly matters is the Judge of all things at the end of every person's life.

> *When we learn to live for God's eyes only, a big weight drops off our shoulders: the unbearable weight of what people will think.*

> For the word of God is living and powerful, and sharper than any two-edged sword, piercing even to the division of soul and spirit, and of joints and marrow, and is a discerner of the thoughts and intents of the heart. And there is no creature hidden from His sight, but all things are naked and open to the eyes of Him to whom we must give account. (Hebrews 4:12–13)

I'm glad that God sees everything and knows everything, but I still tried to hide from Him until He began to teach me that He wants to clean my closet. He's not embarrassed about us, and He doesn't want us to be ashamed. What a wonderful Savior!

I was transferred as a supervisor to a different office when I worked for the postal service, and one of the clerks was obviously trying to impress me when he told me that he was doing Bible study with his son who was in the military. After I had been there a couple of weeks, I walked out to the back dock, and I saw him smoking a cigarette. He was very embarrassed, and he put the cigarette behind his back. He looked sheepish and said, "Oh, you're not supposed to see this." I said, "Who am I that I would matter? I'm not your judge, but the One who judges already knows and sees it, and He still loves you. Talk to Him about it." No one can clean you up like Jesus. It's much better to have Him do it than someone else.

When we live to please men, it causes us to think we're safe if people don't discover our shortcomings, and we end up hiding from God. We become people like this: "Therefore

When we live to please men, it causes us to think we're safe if people don't discover our shortcomings, and we end up hiding from God.

the Lord said: 'Inasmuch as these people draw near with their mouths and honor Me with their lips, but have removed their hearts far from Me, and their fear toward Me is taught by the commandment of men'" (Isaiah 29:13). Instead, this should be our attitude: "But as we have been approved by God to be entrusted with the gospel, even so we speak, not as pleasing men, but God who tests our hearts" (1 Thessalonians 2:4).

CLEAN THE INSIDE OF YOUR CUP FIRST

Jesus sternly warned the religious leaders of the day:

> Woe to you, scribes and Pharisees, hypocrites! For you cleanse the outside of the cup and dish, but inside they are full of extortion and self-indulgence. Blind Pharisee, first cleanse the inside of the cup and dish, that the outside of them may be clean also" (Matthew 23:25–26).

How do we clean the inside of our cup — our inner thoughts? Jesus said that the words we speak come out from inside the heart. We clean up by asking God in His kindness to reveal what is stored in our hearts. He can show us clearly what deep need we are trying to meet through inappropriate means. When He makes it clear, we can genuinely repent and choose His way instead. We can say, "I'm sorry! Please fill me with Your love and peace Your way." This feels so good and clean! It's better to ask Him to clean the inward parts of you than try to keep up appearances before people. When your heart is clean, your words will also come out clean.

"Behold, You desire truth in the inward parts, and in the hidden part You will make me to know wisdom" (Psalm 51:6).

"The sacrifices of God are a broken spirit, a broken and a contrite heart — these, O God, You will not despise" (Psalm 51:17).

In an early step toward the New Testament life, King David learned that God wants the inside person more than the outer sacrifices and offerings. God called David "a man after My own heart" because he wanted his heart to be unified with God very intimately. Do you want to be closer to God? The way is simpler than you think. Make it your project to get your heart as close to Him as you can. Talk to Him about everything.

CLEAN UP RESENTMENT AND UNFORGIVENESS

When He asks us to clean up the dirty closet, it might be surprising what He asks us to do first. Very often, He'll start with resentment and unforgiveness. Even as Christians, we might avoid hating people, and we might not want to get rid of them, but we do resent some people. I found myself reserving the right to resent many people. I did not like some people at all, and I didn't even pray for their good. As I shared in chapter 3, I identified twenty-six people I needed to forgive and stop resenting. Forgiving them all set me free to more easily hear from God and receive His love. My faith had room to function, and my Christian walk became more natural and free-flowing.

If God said to you that you resented someone, who would that person be? Do you have a quick answer? If so, ask God what attitude He would rather you have.

WALK IN THE LIGHT FOR FELLOWSHIP WITH GOD

How do we have fellowship with God? It's not by doing everything right; it's by talking to Him about everything. For example, if I find myself resenting someone, I talk to God about it. I let Him into my thoughts — even the petty or fearful ones. Then I am in fellowship with Him, even before I fix the problem. Because I am sharing with Him, I am being cleansed and helped. If I don't share with Him, I am hiding from His goodness and His help.

> This is the message which we have heard from Him and declare to you, that God is light and in Him is no darkness at all. If we say that we have fellowship with Him, and walk in darkness, we lie and do not practice the truth. But if we walk in the light as He is in the light, we have fellowship with one another, and the blood of Jesus Christ His Son cleanses us from all sin. (1 John 1:5-7)

It is interesting to note how John summed up God's message through His Son to mankind. "God is light and in Him is no darkness at all." There is no place for hiding things in my dirty closet. To have fellowship with Him, I must come out into the light. He didn't say if we never do anything wrong and always do things right then God has fellowship with us. No. He said when we walk in the light. If I cherish any darkness in myself, I need to be ready to come out into the light about it with Him. Did you ever dream how nice it would be to be able to unburden your soul to someone? I found our Savior to be that someone! After I learned that He does not stop loving me because I've been evil, selfish, or proud, I was able to come to Him in the light and plainly talk to Him.

We all have a deep desire for this kind of honesty and openness. We want to be united with someone willing to be open in sharing and receiving honest communication. Husbands and wives want this. Parents desire it from their children. As parents, we wish our children would talk to us about their struggles so we can help them before they make a big mistake. And when they do make a mistake, we would prefer they tell us what they did wrong, rather than try to hide it. We know if they hide it and keep it inside themselves, it will grow like a disease. We must begin this practice of coming into the light with God, and then we will be able to do it with people. I can testify that this really happens!

COME TO THE LIGHT FOR FREEDOM

Walking in the light is a wonderful experience, and it will make a greater difference in your life than you think. Notice the pressure, grief, and groaning the Psalmist felt before he came into the light with God:

> Blessed is he whose transgression is forgiven, whose sin is covered. Blessed is the man to whom the LORD does not impute iniquity, and in whose spirit there is no deceit. When I kept silent, my bones grew old through my groaning all the day long. For day and night Your hand was heavy upon me; my vitality was turned into the drought of summer. Selah. I acknowledged my sin to You, and my iniquity I have not hidden. I said, "I will confess my transgressions to the LORD," and You forgave the iniquity of my sin. Selah. (Psalm 32:1–5)

See how the pent-up problem inside his soul and heart kept growing and putting more pressure on him as long as he kept it in the dark? When he finally confessed (v. 5), God forgave the iniquity of his sin.

After having learned to walk in the light, and I was practicing it, I said to my oldest daughter, "You know I talk plainly to God about my darkest, most embarrassing thoughts and actions. Do you want to do that too?" I saw the fear on her face. She said, "Ouch, do I really want to do that? It sounds very painful!" Yes, it is painful when you begin. It took a while before she began to do it, and she was happy when she did because it brings such a sweet fellowship with God.

It is so freeing to the soul to know that God will hear, that He already knows, and that He's happy to cleanse us from all unrighteousness. Come experience Him more intimately by walking in the light with the Lover of Your Soul.

> *It is so freeing to the soul to know that God will hear, that He already knows, and that He's happy to cleanse us from all unrighteousness.*

"I want to help you clean out your dirty closet so you won't be ashamed."

— *Jesus, in a word to Jim Kaminski*

CHAPTER 10

Live Daily for God

Experiencing Spiritual Growth Through Small Actions

We all know the frustration when the afterglow drains out too soon after we attend big, wonderful, "life-changing" meetings. Two weeks later, we can't remember anything that was taught, and we're not really changed. Happily, Jesus guaranteed our personal growth in the same way farmers plant seeds.

> And He said, "The kingdom of God is as if a man should scatter seed on the ground, and should sleep by night and rise by day, and the seed should sprout and grow, he himself does not know how. For the earth yields crops by itself: first the blade, then the head, after that the full grain in the head. But when the grain ripens, immediately he puts in the sickle, because the harvest has come." (Mark 4:26–29)

Notice the farmer doesn't know how it happens, and he just goes on with his daily life. He is even oblivious to its growth because some of it happens while he is asleep. How would you like to grow even when you are asleep? Jesus said it happens in the kingdom of God! The earth brings forth by itself, as our version here says. The word in the original Greek text is *auto-mate* and sounds like our word *automatic*. He's speaking of your heart, your soul, your life. The Word of God sown in you will automatically bear fruit. It happens in small ways and can be almost imperceptible to you.

> **The Word of God sown in you will automatically bear fruit.**

A PASTOR'S A-TO-Z PRAYER LIST CHANGED ME

I heard that my Pastor T. in Flagstaff, Arizona, was praying for everyone in the church by name. He listed them A-to-Z and divided them up into the seven days of the week. I thought that I could do that also. As I prayed for them daily, something happened to me. I began to love them like I never had before.

I began praying with people who needed cars, and they started getting them. When I prayed with one man who needed a car, he received one worth five times his yearly income! Then everyone said, "Oh, go talk to Jim, and he will pray with you." I became the "pray with me to get a car" guy!

I was unknowingly developing a pastor's heart through my daily prayers. After some months, Pastor T. and his wife called my wife and me up to the podium to anoint us and call us out as pastors. Even though I did not necessarily see the change in myself, it was happening, and others confirmed it.

God is doing this in you, too. You are growing and changing, even by reading this book. Showing up for your loved ones, reading the Bible, and praying for others are robust seeds growing you up to look more and more like Jesus, the Author and Finisher of your faith.

THIS IS NOT FAR AWAY FROM YOU

"But the hour is coming, and now is, when true worshipers will worship the Father in spirit and in truth; for the Father is seeking such to worship Him. God is Spirit, and those who worship Him must worship in spirit and truth" (John 4:23–24). Jesus said to worship everywhere: in your mountain, my mountain, any mountain, no mountain. Just like the air is always there for us to breathe, connecting with God is always available because His Spirit is everywhere.

Do you only pray on Sunday in church? If we only pray on Sunday at church, it's because we believe that God's kingdom place is only there. If we think that when we're at home that's not kingdom time, then we will not be apt to pray. The mistake happens when we only pray when we're in church. You'd like to hear from your kids. Do you only hear from them at special times and places? Wouldn't you prefer to hear from them often? Doesn't God desire to hear from you often as well?

IT'S POSSIBLE TO PRAY
WITHOUT CEASING

An American pastor went to Africa to preach and teach, and the church there was happy to have him. There was a lady listening to him as he was talking about praying without ceasing

(1Thessalonians 5:17). He said, "I don't know anybody who prays without ceasing, or how anybody can. Does anybody out there know how to pray without ceasing?" This little servant lady put her hand up, and he said, "Yes, what is it?" She said, "I'm a servant at a house. I'm happy to have that job. When I'm washing dishes, I'm saying, 'God wash my heart and wash my soul.' When I'm preparing food, I pray, 'God prepare the daily manna for me and in all the things I do.' Every day, everything I do reminds me to talk to God."

EVERYTHING IS OR CAN BE KINGDOM ACTIVITY

I heard a story from one Christian leader who said he was having his God time all by himself in the quiet of the morning when his two-year-old awakened. His wife was sick, so he had to interrupt his God time to go feed the baby. Did you hear anything strange in that story? He thought that his God time was over because he wasn't sitting there with his Bible. Do you wonder what Jesus thought? Maybe he thought this: "And whoever gives one of these little ones only a cup of cold water in the name of a disciple, assuredly, I say to you, he shall not lose his reward" (Matthew 10:42). Jesus thought that was kingdom-of-God activity. This man doubted he was doing God's will at the time, and he was needlessly frustrated because of a false idea.

It's helpful to have the intention that everything we're doing is kingdom activity. This comes from what the Apostle Paul said: "And whatever you do in word or deed, do all in the name of the Lord Jesus, giving thanks to God the Father through Him" (Colossians 3:17).

When I was a new believer, a Christian friend told me a story that had impressed him, and I have not forgotten it. His neighbor, a mature Christian man, awakened early each morning to remove one neighbor's dog poop from another neighbor's lawn. He explained his reason to my Christian friend: he did it because he didn't want his two neighbors to argue with each other over the situation. It was not his dog, not his yard, and not his responsibility, but he took up the task to sow love and peace among his neighbors. These small kindnesses gave the Holy Spirit room to grow divine love and wisdom in his heart.

NO "CLASS" IS WASTED BY THE HOLY SPIRIT

How many of you went to college or even high school and took a bunch of classes you haven't used? It's frustrating to think you might never use them. In all my years of work, I think I've used twelve hours of the math I took in college. I used them to qualify as a math tutor when I needed extra money. You never know how God will weave together those random times in our lives.

In your life, in your story, the Holy Spirit will not waste any experience. A friend of mine named Jerry is a counselor, and he told me, "For every person I encounter, God says there's something for you to learn and receive from them, and something for them to learn and receive from you." What a great attitude! "Lord, what do you want me to do and what do you want to have done to me because I have met and experienced this person?"

> *In your life, in your story, the Holy Spirit will not waste any experience.*

Do you feel like you failed some of God's classes learning patience or humility? If you failed a class in college, what did you do? You just took it again because it was required. Your class in humility or joy or prayer or other virtues is a required class. If you fail it, you know what? Just sign up again. "God, I'm signing up again for Your humility class and Your prayer class. I want to learn these. I want to go for it again. I want to take these classes until I pass." How about it? I would love to hear that many of you are doing that.

Again, daily living is your easy-to-implement improvement plan. Daily living, with some of these disciplines and these attitudes, is guaranteed by the law of seed growth to get you off the plateau in your Christian life. Jesus said the seed grows by day and night; the farmer doesn't even know how or why. Your life, too, will grow as you engage with Him in the experiences He is bringing you every day. Pay attention to the small daily things in life. It will be wonderful.

What are some new spaces you can make in your life to plant seeds for spiritual growth? What daily practice impressed you when you saw it in a pastor, leader, or mentor? You, as God's child, have access to the same empowering Holy Spirit who knows how to work in you and help you develop in a new way. Now is the time to take a step and implement something new and quietly powerful in your life.

"There's so much daily living that it must be very important!"

— *Jim Kaminski*

CHAPTER *11*

Surrender It All
Because He Is Worth It

Sacrificing Your Desires for His Kingdom

As I was studying the Lord's Prayer one day, I saw that Jesus said to pray, "Your kingdom come. Your will be done on earth as it is in heaven" (Matthew 6:10). I asked the Lord a question. "Which kingdom might I be serving more than Yours? I know that thing is likely hindering me. Is it the world, my boss, money, fame, my favorite sports team? Which of these kingdoms is hindering Yours the most?" And I received an answer quickly from Him. He said, "Oh, that would be Jim's kingdom."

That hit me deeply. I saw that I had changes to make. I began to examine and identify how much I was serving my own kingdom. I was shocked to discover how much I was doing that made me happy, safe, or honored. These were places where my desires were crowding His out. If you've come this far in this book, you've already passed through some of the things that have been holding you back. And one of the last things that holds you back is simply your own kingdom.

> **One of the last things that holds you back is simply your own kingdom.**

Through parables, Jesus taught that it is worth selling all you own to gain the kingdom of heaven.

> Again, the kingdom of heaven is like treasure hidden in a field, which a man found and hid; and for joy over it he goes and sells all that he has and buys that field. Again, the kingdom of heaven is like a merchant seeking beautiful pearls, who, when he had found one pearl of great price, went and sold all that he had and bought it. (Matthew 13:44–46)

Many understand that people are the treasure in the field, and Jesus paid all He had to purchase them. This agrees with another parable where Jesus compared the field to the world. It is a beautiful truth that Jesus's sacrifice demonstrated His unlimited love by giving all He was and all He had to purchase us.

The pearl of great price is usually thought to be Christ Himself and the need to sell all for Him. How do you know that you have chosen Jesus as your Master? Find the answer by asking: How much did it cost me to belong to Him? Have I given up my rights to do whatever I want in deference and reverence and love for Jesus?

In Luke chapter 14, Jesus claims that no one is worthy of Him who doesn't forsake everything he has.

> For which of you, intending to build a tower, does not sit down first and count the cost, whether he

has enough to finish it — lest, after he has laid the foundation, and is not able to finish, all who see it begin to mock him, saying, 'This man began to build and was not able to finish'? Or what king, going to make war against another king, does not sit down first and consider whether he is able with ten thousand to meet him who comes against him with twenty thousand? Or else, while the other is still a great way off, he sends a delegation and asks conditions of peace. So likewise, whoever of you does not forsake all that he has cannot be My disciple. (Luke 14:28–33)

Is He going a bit too far with this? I hear Him saying He is worth more than everything I have. No mere human could demand this. Think about it. What might motivate you to sell your house and move out of town? Have you done it before for a job or for your child? What was the situation? If you've already done it for human love, then you would do it in like manner for your worthy Savior Jesus.

EARTHLY FOOD VS. HEAVENLY FOOD

Jesus often challenged the motives of His followers. In John chapter 6, after feeding thousands, He confronted their priorities. He went across the lake in a boat. They all came over there looking for Him, and He asked (author's paraphrase), "What are you guys doing over here?" They said, "Well, we heard You came over here, Master." And Jesus said, "You know you came over here not because you saw the miracles but because you were fed." His statement in John 6:27 is still good today: "Do not labor for the food which perishes, but for the food which endures to everlasting life, which the Son of Man will give you, because God the Father has set His seal on Him."

We read that in the Garden of Eden, Adam and Eve chose to be supplied by an earthly tree instead of the heavenly Tree of Life. Jesus said in other places, including the Sermon on the Mount, that our earthly food is supplied by our Father in heaven and to not be anxious or worried about it. Check your priorities. Do you make sure to eat God's Word as regularly as you eat three meals a day? Are you hungry to read your Bible? Now might be a good time to start a new diet, knowing the new food will be nourishing, fulfilling, and eternal.

Jesus's lesson is that what we really need and must attend to is the spiritual food. "Then Jesus said to them, 'Most assuredly, I say to you, Moses did not give you the bread from heaven, but My Father gives you the true bread from heaven. For the bread of God is He who comes down from heaven and gives life to the world'" (John 6:32–33).

Have you ever realized that your salvation is a *Person*? "And this is the testimony: that God has given us eternal life, and this life is in His Son" (1 John 5:11). The Apostle Paul learned that Jesus Himself is the real heavenly food, and he expounded on this in his epistles.

> *Have you ever realized that your salvation is a Person?*

PAUL KNEW THE DEEP RICHES OF KNOWING CHRIST

When I read Paul's words in Philippians chapter 3, I'm very impressed with how he had forsaken everything for Christ. Notice what Paul *wants*:

> But what things were gain to me, these I have
> counted loss for Christ. Yet indeed I also count
> all things loss for the excellence of the knowl-
> edge of Christ Jesus my Lord, for whom I have
> suffered the loss of all things, and count them
> as rubbish, that I may gain Christ and be found
> in Him, not having my own righteousness,
> which is from the law, but that which is through
> faith in Christ, the righteousness which is from
> God by faith; that I may know Him and the
> power of His resurrection, and the fellowship of
> His sufferings, being conformed to His death.
> (Philippians 3:7–10)

Notice Paul was not even sad about anything he gave up. As a matter of fact, he said even the things he thought were helpful were trash compared to knowing Christ.

I read that, and I ask myself, do I have that attitude about knowing Christ? I'm asking you to think about that too. Paul prays above "that I may know Him and the power of his resur-rection, and the fellowship of His sufferings, being conformed to His death." There's a prayer for me and you!

Paul wrote this from the prison in Rome, where he probably thought his life would end. And this is what he wanted to say to God's people. Jesus did not write this. It was written by Paul, a man whom Christ saved and who became a Christian like you. He asserts (author's paraphrase), "I want to know Christ more. I want to know Him as thoroughly as I possibly can. And I've come to count everything junk except knowing Him."

Forsaking yourself and the self-life looks tough! This is perhaps the final frontier, if you want to call it that, to finding and knowing the life of God that is in Christ. Jesus said, "For I came down from heaven, not to do My own will, but the will of

Him who sent Me" (John 6:38). And so it is with us. In Matthew chapter 19, Jesus asked a man to give up all his money to follow Him. The disciples objected that it was difficult. Pointing to necessary power from God, Jesus said, "With men this is impossible, but with God all things are possible" (Matthew 19:26).

As Paul said, I've been apprehended by Christ, and I want to apprehend what I've been apprehended for. We're invited to have this attitude. God is not looking for perfection, but for pursuit. The treasure of Christ is available to anyone willing to give all. Will you sell all and follow Him? This request and offer repeat every day of our lives. Christ gave everything for you, and He asks you to give everything for Him. He promises it as a lovely, wonderful life. Let's go get Him!

"And you will seek Me and find Me, when you search for Me with all your heart. I will be found by you, says the LORD."

— Jeremiah 29:13-14

CHAPTER *12*

Embrace Your New Life

Understanding What New Covenant Living Looks Like

In chapter 1, I told you about the time I said to God, "I won't be praying to You anymore the rest of my life." Then five years later, I was closer than ever to God, having daily joy, and praying ten times as much as I had before. How did that happen? Why did my spiritual life not crash and burn as Satan intended?

One monumental reason I survived and then thrived was because, as in chapter 2, I had identified some of the systemic lies that are widely believed in the church. I had found those and gotten rid of them. One of the most destructive lies I overcame was that I have a bad or evil heart. One of the best truths I came to know was that God gave me a good heart. This made a huge difference for me in all the undergirding of my Christian life. I was generally healthier as a Christian because of this. I returned to knowing that God is my Friend, my Helper, my Deliverer, and my Counselor.

One of the very first things I had to do after the huge loss of my precious wife was reinterpret my understanding of the loss, as outlined in chapter 3. As I reviewed that situation, I learned not to blame God for it, and not even to blame myself or my wife. This opened the door for me to start to pray again, and to learn to pray better, because I wasn't blaming God now (which always causes a problem!).

Then I began reaffirming God as my Source and moving from how-to to who-to, as I related in chapter 4. I knew that God wanted me to be personally talking with Him. Over time, I learned to hear God's voice better. Understanding that He speaks to me at least once a day encouraged me to readily talk to Him and expect to hear His voice, as discussed in chapter 5.

Next, I clarified how important it is to follow Abraham by walking my promised land to picture it, as explained in chapter 6. I saw that following the law could not give me entrance into the promised land, but Jesus could. The wonderful promises from Jeremiah and Ezekiel of a new heart (mentioned in chapter 7) thrilled me and set me free from laboring under the misconceptions that I still had a hard, stubborn heart and couldn't be pleasing to God.

I recounted in chapter 8 that Jesus plainly stated He came to be an inside Christ. What amazing salvation God has prepared for us, that He is not far away but insists on being inside us! "For we are to God the fragrance of Christ" (2 Corinthians 2:15). Consider this: Father God smells the beautiful aroma of His Son in you! All these understandings added together gave me enough power to make it through and then, ultimately, thrive when the worst tempest came.

When you learn to make a full disclosure with Christ of your secret dirty laundry, it gives a freedom in your soul you never thought was possible. This undertaking I described in chapter 9. Please ask God for grace to do this. It is not easily begun, but it is certainly worth it.

Remember from chapter 10 that you grow steadily through small daily practices. You don't often sense your progress until you look back at the old attitudes you once held. "Therefore be patient, brethren, until the coming of the Lord. See how the farmer waits for the precious fruit of the earth, waiting patiently for it until it receives the early and latter rain" (James 5:7). God confronted me regarding my ideas for my own "kingdom of Jim" and called me to seek His kingdom and His self. Chapter 11 communicates this great calling to live for Him. "You did not choose Me, but I chose you and appointed you that you should go and bear fruit, and that your fruit should remain, that whatever you ask the Father in My name He may give you" (John 15:16).

My concern for people who are plateaued in their Christian life comes because I fear they will not have the power necessary to survive difficult trials, which come to us all. My mission is to encourage you to walk these steps that I've outlined in the previous chapters so that you will be strong and able to stand, as in Ephesians chapter 6. We need to have on all the armor of God so that we'll be able to withstand the evil day and to stay standing. Fastening on the belt of truth gets rid of the lies that we have learned. Accepting the breastplate of righteousness makes us confident in our hearts that we are right with God. The sword of the Spirit, which is the Word of God, deals with the attacks on our well-being. When we put up our shield of faith instead of relying on our own strength, we defeat our spiritual enemy. If you've read this book and taken to heart what's in these chapters, it will help you stand when an evil day comes.

Some of the stories related in this book attest to my walking through shocking losses and times of plateaued Christian living. Through these, our Lord has graciously led me to know Jesus more when I needed Him more. Because of this, I labor in prayer for you all until Christ is formed in you.

He is the One who causes you to thrive during pain and plateaus. Your daily living in Him, keeping your eyes on your present promised land, hearing from God, and letting Him clean you out add up to strength when the storms come. You will be firm on the Rock, and your new life will look different. It will look like peace, confidence, a conversational prayer life, and more.

PEACE

Our new life does not look like checking obedience levels frequently to see if God is happy with us. It doesn't look like I'm keeping Hellfire insurance in force by good works, going to church, and giving and doing many outward things. Instead, it's a life of peace He freely gives.

It's also Jeremiah 29:11–13, where God says,

> For I know the thoughts that I think toward you... thoughts of peace and not of evil, to give you a future and a hope. Then you will call upon Me and go and pray to Me, and I will listen to you. And you will seek Me and find Me, when you search for Me with all your heart.

This connection to God is foundational to our peace. We search for Him with all our heart, and we will be one of those people who walk around with peace during a storm. Our current problem might be too big for us, but it's not too big for us and Him together. If our children get into bad company, we

We will be one of those people who walk around with peace during a storm.

have this confidence and peace that God gives us the resources to deal with it. Sometimes our children choose to wander away from God, and many of us have shared this burden of the soul. Our children may take a "world tour," but through prayer and the supply of the Spirit of God, we trust they will return.

"I have no rights to claim, no honor to defend, and no revenge to seek." As we recite this as often as needed, these attitudes will grow, and we'll increase in peacefulness. Be quick to forgive anyone who has brought pain.

CONFIDENCE

New Covenant living also looks like positive access to God. It's a real living boldness. Hebrews 10:19–23 gives us the reasons we have it:

> Therefore, brethren, having boldness to enter the Holiest by the blood of Jesus, by a new and living way which He consecrated for us, through the veil, that is, His flesh, and having a High Priest over the house of God, let us draw near with a true heart in full assurance of faith, having our hearts sprinkled from an evil conscience and our bodies washed with pure water. Let us hold fast the confession of our hope without wavering, for He who promised is faithful.

We see and feel this boldness in thoughts like "Because of Christ's blood, I know God is always willing to commune with me," or "I have an inside Christ." We also have the sense that our Big Brother, Jesus, is always with us. He's always here, and nobody can bully us with the fears they're trying to give us.

Do we spend too much time worrying about being conformed to the image of Christ? Be assured that God wants this more than we do. The Holy Spirit is ready, willing, and able to do this.

CONVERSATIONAL PRAYER LIFE

New Covenant life is also reflected in our conversations with God. It's not having trouble praying, feeling unable to pray, being afraid to pray in public, or knowing what to pray. Instead, we come to the place where it's just a conversation with God — a two-way conversation with Him about everything, anything, all our thoughts. Sometimes people say to me, "I don't know how to pray." And my response is, "Yes, you do. You just talked to me, and you can talk to Him just like that. Simple. He understands you."

I know the Teacher lives inside me, and I tend to ask Him any kind of question that comes up in my mind. I ask Him before Google, or instead of Google entirely. We know God is the One who knows everything. Why not ask Him and talk to Him? We can learn to love doing that, and our conversations with God will take on new meaning.

DAILY KINGDOM-OF-HEAVEN LIVING

Begin to wake up in the morning and ask, "Lord Jesus, what's Your kingdom agenda today? Do you want me to get that flat tire fixed? Help that widow with some painting? Listen to the neighbor who has some new problems? What does your kingdom want today? Not my kingdom but Yours." Pray, "Our Father in heaven. Hallowed be Your name, Your kingdom come. Your will be done on earth as it is in heaven."

The Holy Spirit is someone who flows through you, as Jesus said in John 7:38, "He who believes in Me, as the Scripture has said, out of his heart will flow rivers of living water." Rivers of living water will begin to come out of you, and people will come to you. More and more will start calling you, talking to you, wanting to know if you'll pray with them or what you think about things, because Jesus said this about the Holy Spirit. The Holy Spirit is in you, and talking with Him is a daily experience. As you come alive, people will notice.

STRENGTH AFTER TRIALS

Peter says in 1 Peter 5:10, "But may the God of all grace, who called us to His eternal glory by Christ Jesus, after you have suffered a while, perfect, establish, strengthen, and settle you." You'll notice that even though you have suffered — and we've talked about some suffering and some hard times in this book — He has begun perfecting, establishing, strengthening, and settling you. The fruit of the Spirit is more and more evident in your life: "love, joy, peace, longsuffering, kindness, goodness, faithfulness, gentleness, self-control. Against such there is no law" (Galatians 5:22–23).

NEARNESS TO GOD

In this new life, there's also a nearness to God. Being close to God is not thinking, "Well, Christ is the one I trust mainly when it's time to die, and I know I'll go to be with Him." It's a narrative with Him continually. Every day, you begin to believe you are already in your promised land because being with Him is your promised land. In Luke 15:31, the father said to the elder son, "Son, you are always with me, and all that I have is yours." You begin to know that you are always with your Heavenly Father. Sonship begins to be everything that matters to you.

I used to be bothered about the amount of money I had, the amount of debt I had, the amount of business I had, my work, how people acted, how people treated me, and how my family treated me. When the kingdom of God is the priority, those things don't bother you anymore.

Jesus said, "And this is eternal life, that they may know You, the only true God, and Jesus Christ whom You have sent" (John 17:3). Our eternal life has already started, according to John 5:24, and eternal life consists of knowing God the Father and knowing Jesus Christ. That becomes enough.

Of all the things discussed in this book, listening to your Shepherd's voice is the most important. Hear Him speaking to you in the Scriptures. Discuss everything happening in your soul and heart, and you'll find that He has a word in season for you.

> *Of all the things discussed in this book, listening to your Shepherd's voice is the most important.*

WHAT DOES LOVE LOOK LIKE?

The life of Jesus in us makes a wonderful difference. Flowers are more beautiful, the sky bluer, and the plants greener. Little children are more precious. Daily living is done in peace alongside Jesus. Servanthood is a peaceful, delightful lifestyle. We don't mind being behind the scenes. We even regard difficult people as wandering sheep, trying to find their way, and we know there's a loving Creator-Savior for them. The love of God that has filled our hearts is stronger than all the resistance and selfishness of men.

Above everything and everyone on earth, Christ is all.

"But you, beloved, building yourselves up on your most holy faith, praying in the Holy Spirit, *keep yourselves in the love of God*, looking for the mercy of our Lord Jesus Christ unto eternal life" (Jude 1:20-21, emphasis added).

I've written this book to tell you some of the things that Jesus has done for me and for others, with the hope that you may believe that He is your Savior through times of pain and plateau and that He brings you into your promised land — all because He wants to bring you *closer to Him.*

"Now may the God of peace Himself sanctify you completely;
and may your whole spirit, soul, and body be preserved
blameless at the coming of our Lord Jesus Christ.
He who calls you is faithful, who also will do it."

— 1 Thessalonians 5:23-24

Invitation to New Covenant Life

If this book has opened your eyes to the beauty and freedom of New Covenant living, I want you to know — this is only the beginning. I invite you to something further.

Come closer still. Help is available.

I believe this message is too powerful to keep to ourselves. Join our community of believers who are learning to walk in the freedom, peace, and power of the New Covenant life. We offer online gatherings, Christ-centered resources, and training opportunities, and we are accomplishing the vision to certify New Covenant life coaches in every US state to share this message of freedom and rest.

**Learn more, sign up for event updates,
or join our online community at:**

NewCovenantLife.com

Let's keep going — closer to God and fully alive in Him.

— *Jim Kaminski*

New Covenant Life Words of Wisdom

▶ What is hindering your increase in God is not a mystery.

▶ Canceling religious lies produced the biggest increase in my life with God.

▶ In the parable of the wedding feast invitation (Luke 14:15–24), notice all three men rejected God's invitation to dine with His Son based on a busyness excuse. This ought to concern us.

▶ If each of us really listened to our soul, we would know with certainty that, yes, we want more than "safe" with God.

▶ Trials come with your choice to swallow a lie or to grow in God.

▶ There is always someone else who has had the same problem as you. If you can talk with that person, do!

▸ You do not have to wait for anyone in your life to change before you can draw nearer to God.

▸ I was created in the image of and by a Who, not a how-to. That's why my life transformation was to depend on a Who, and to become a who that I wasn't before. I did not become a how-to, but I became a who.

▸ If you're not hearing God's voice, it's because somebody talked you out of it.

▸ The Holy Spirit is the delivery person of God's voice.

▸ Your promised land is the life of fruitfulness, intimacy, and impact God wants you to live right now — not just someday in heaven.

▸ Moses's failure to enter is the picture of our trying hard under our own power to gain our promised land.

▸ Jesus is commissioned to cause God's people to enter their promised land.

▸ Many Christians struggle not because they lack sincerity, but because they try to live the Christian life with Old Covenant methods instead of New Covenant realities.

▸ God makes it natural for us as branches to draw in life from the vine and put out fruit through ourselves.

▸ Jesus plainly stated that He came to be an inside Christ.

▸ The knowledge of Christ needed for initial salvation does not suffice for continued growth in Christ.

▸ When we learn to live for God's eyes only, a big weight drops off our shoulders: the unbearable weight of what people will think.

▸ When we live to please men, it causes us to think we're safe if people don't discover our secrets, and we end up hiding from God.

▸ It's better to ask Him to clean the inward parts of you than try to keep up appearances before people.

▸ Did you ever dream how nice it would be to be able to unburden your soul to someone? I found our Savior to be that someone!

▸ It is so freeing to the soul to know that God will hear, that He already knows, and that He's happy to cleanse us from all unrighteousness.

▸ One of the last things that holds you back is simply your own kingdom.

▸ There's so much daily living that it must be very important!

▸ The Word of God sown in you will automatically bear fruit.

▸ In your life, in your story, the Holy Spirit will not waste any experience.

▸ God: "My people are serving Me out of duty. I want them to serve Me out of love."

▸ The promised land is that place in God where you think it's too hard for you to enter.

▸ Paul said in Galatians 4:19, "My little children, for whom I labor in birth again until Christ is formed in you." There is a formation of Christ in us that happens subsequent to receiving Christ.

▸ Romans chapter 6 says twelve different ways that we are dead to sin, freed from sin, and alive to God.

▸ The Holy Spirit is able to conform you to the image of the beloved Son. He's willing to do it, and He's actively doing it.

▸ When you have entered God's rest, you will be one of those people who walk around with peace during the storm.

▸ Of all the things discussed in this book, listening to your Shepherd's voice is the most important.

▸ Have you ever realized that your salvation is a Person? (1 John 5:11; John 6:33)

Endnotes

1   John C. Maxwell, *The 15 Invaluable Laws of Growth: Live Them and Reach Your Potential* (New York: Center Street, 2012), 3.

2   Brent Curtis and John Eldredge, *The Sacred Romance: Drawing Closer to the Heart of God* (Nashville, TN: Thomas Nelson, 1997).

3   Andrew Murray, *Like Christ: Thoughts on the Blessed Life of Conformity to the Son of God* (Chicago: F.H. Revell, 2018).

4   Gene Edwards, *Crucified by Christians* (Jacksonville, FL: SeedSowers Christian Publishing, 2015).

5   Andrew Murray, *Absolute Surrender* (Minneapolis: Bethany House, 2003).

6   Malcolm Boyd, *Are You Running with Me, Jesus? Prayers by Malcolm Boyd* (New York: Holt, Rinehart, and Winston, 1965).

7   Brother Lawrence, *The Practice of the Presence of God* (New Kensington, PA: Whitaker House, 1982).

8   Leonard Ravenhill, "The Judgment Seat of Christ," *OnePlace*, accessed May 28, 2025, https://www.oneplace.com/ministries/leonard-ravenhill/read/articles/the-judgment-seat-of-christ-16552.html.

9   Charles G. Finney, "Lecture LXIII: Sanctification," *Lectures on Systematic Theology*, The Gospel Truth, accessed June 11, 2025, https://www.gospeltruth.net/1847ST/1847st_lec63.htm.

10 Andrew Murray, *Within or The Kingdom of God Is Within You* (Mansfield Centre, CT: Martino Publishing, 2012), 75–76.

11 Andrew Murray, *The Holiest of All* (Springdale, PA: Whitaker House, 1996).

12 Robert Boyd Munger, *My Heart–Christ's Home*, rev. ed. (Downers Grove, IL: InterVarsity Press, 1986).

Acknowledgements

I thank Our Lord Jesus Christ, who created me, keeps me, loves me, redeems me, and has become my Life. Without You, I can do nothing.

I must express my deepest gratitude to my wife, Bertha, for her steadfast love and unwavering support throughout this long and challenging writing process. Her comments contributed much to this book. "Who can find a virtuous wife? For her worth is far above rubies" (Proverbs 31:10).

God used all my beautiful, loving children to keep me going. They are truly arrows in the hand of a mighty man.

I am greatly indebted to my daughter Angela Dubin for her editing. She moved this project along and provided much technical savvy, along with my son-in-law Michael Dubin, who provided text review and a lifetime of enlightening discussions about Scripture.

My son Dave Kaminski and his wife Marilyn Kaminski gave me the vision, the push, and the blessing I needed to begin this work and to finish it. Without you, no book!

My son Aaron Kaminski and his wife Angela Kaminski, daughter Alisha Anderson and her husband Paul Anderson, and son Michael Kaminski and his wife Kim Kaminski all demonstrate a family living in love and respect for God and for one another. This atmosphere is like heaven on earth. All of them make me feel important as Dad. I am grateful to my wonderful granddaughters Charissa Juarez and Melissa Hahnke for transcribing my original recorded sermons on these topics. I trust that each of them will be writing her own books in the future.

This book could not have been possible without the visionary guidance of Nicole Gebhardt, Kim Han, and the great crew at Niche Pressworks. They brought me the amazing team I knew I needed throughout the entire writing and publishing process from A to Z. That includes my editor, Abby, who understood the vision of the book and provided helpful structure, organization, and a keen eye to bring it to completion.

My deepest thanks to Deonna Kaminski, my wife of thirty-two years, who loved souls fiercely and put up with me for so long. Now she has entered her reward.

I thank my pastors and every pastor who gives their life to watch for souls. Keep going. Many more need your important sacrifices.

To all my readers, wherever you are: you are the ones I see in my mind as I endeavor in prayer until Christ be formed in you.

About the Author

Jim Kaminski was born in Illinois in 1951, the sixth of ten children in a lively family of seven girls and three boys. He earned a Bachelor of Science in biology with a minor in mathematics from the University of Illinois in 1973, the same year he married his first wife, Deonna, with whom he raised five children. In 1974, Jim and Deonna moved to Arizona, where he pastored churches while also working for the US Postal Service until his retirement in 2004.

A lifelong student of Scripture, Jim also studied Bible theology through distance learning from 1974 to 1987. In 1990, he entered what he describes as God's spiritual rest — a turning point that transformed his walk with Christ. After the loss of his first wife, he married Bertha. Together, they share a blended family of seven children, twenty-three grandchildren, and one great-grandchild.

Jim also served for fourteen years as a school bus driver in Gilbert, Arizona, collecting stories and sharing wisdom along the way. Now living in the Phoenix area, Jim is a prayer intercessor, church group leader, and board member of an African relief agency. He is passionate about raising up others to teach and model New Covenant life — anchored in God's rest, empowered by the Spirit, and grounded in prayer. Influenced by the writings of Andrew Murray and John Eldredge, Jim carries a lifelong vision: that God's house would be a house of prayer and that the Church would fully embrace the New Covenant life of rest promised through Christ.

CONTACT

Website: NewCovenantLife.com
Email: Jim@NewCovenantLife.com